SUCCESS IN SERIES PREACHING

William Goulooze

BV
4223
.G6
1982

BAKER BOOK HOUSE
Grand Rapids, Michigan 49506

Copyright 1956 by
Baker Book House

Mass market edition
issued 1982

Library of Congress
Catalog Card Number: 56-7576

Formerly issued under the
title: 1500 THEMES FOR PREACHING

PHOTOLITHOPRINTED BY CUSHING - MALLOY, INC.
ANN ARBOR, MICHIGAN, UNITED STATES OF AMERICA

TABLE OF CONTENTS

	Page
Introduction	1
I. Word Connected Series	9
II. Idea Connected Series	28
III. Chapter Connected Series	51
IV. Bible Book Series	63
V. Doctrinal Series	75
VI. The Life of Christ Series	90
VII. Lenten Series	102
VIII. Easter Series	110
IX. Advent Series	114
X. Bible Character Series	121
XI. Church History Series	135
XII. Hymn Series	141
XIII. Nature Series	149

PREFACE

It must be remembered in studying the series suggested in this book that they were prepared by the author out of his experience and his study of the Bible. They are not final for anyone. Most of these series have been tested, having been placed into sermons and preached before congregations. The law of variation in the preacher and in types of congregations must always be remembered.

The series are suggested for use, adaptation, suggestion and discovery of other series on the part of the reading minister. These series may be used freely to the glory of God within the limitations set by the copyright privilege.

It is the prayer of the author that they may be a blessing to the minister who prepares them for his people, and for the listening congregation so that all may grow in the grace and knowledge of Jesus Christ and the unsaved may be attracted to our wonderful Saviour for redemption and better living.

William Goulooze

INTRODUCTION

A. How to Build Series of Sermons

The modern minister finds his people clamoring for series of sermons. He either finds delight in satisfying that need or he is in constant turmoil because he lacks the ability to preach series of sermons successfully.

The secret of series sermon preaching lies in the ability to make each sermon a unity, apart by itself, and yet related to the entire series by psychological and spiritual interest. Many ministers fail in the series because they use the introduction of a given sermon to tell about the sermons already preached in the series and the conclusion to tell about the next sermon or sermons to follow. A connecting link in the form of a few remarks may be necessary. However, each sermon should stand as a unity by itself and yet related to the whole, so that when one has heard the particular sermon he will feel the urge to come back to hear the balance of the entire series.

There are specific suggestions for various types of series in addition to the suggestions covering the general principles of serial preaching. Special suggestions will follow in succeeding chapters. This chapter will be devoted to general suggestions for serial preaching.

1. Be on the alert for serial ideas. Watch what others are preaching about and let one series suggest another of similar or different type.

2. Watch for human interest clues on the part of your people as you converse with them. Cultivate an acquaintance with their interests and know their manner of work, relaxation, reading, radio listening and television viewing.

3. Write down any idea of a possible series even though, at the time, you see only one or two texts associated with ideas under the serial caption. File these under the heading of "Possible Series" and allow them to grow as you read, observe and study. See 12 and 13 for detailed explanation.

4. Note carefully associations in your concordance study of Scripture. Many series are born when you study the Word through the use of concordances in relation to word and idea studies.

5. As your series builds in your mind, list your subtopics under the main series topic, and make outlines on cards of the texts to be used in the series. You will avoid overlapping of ideas if you briefly outline the texts with introduction, divisions and conclusion.

6. Allow the series to rest (let it "steep"), and as you come back to it again and again you may shift the order of your proposed subtopics, you may eliminate some and add others. The series will then begin to take shape.

Be sure to make the series, complete with outlines as indicated in 5, before you announce the first sermon of the series. Some ministers announce a series and if it works out well, having a good reception, other subjects are added. Occasionally this may work out, but more often it leads to confusion on the part of the minister and the people as well. There must be progress and a climax in a series and this should be planned in advance of any announcement. To announce a series as a whole gives your people the confidence that you know what you are doing and that there is a purpose in your planning.

7. When you set forth your program for the entire year you can select from your steeping series such as will fit the preaching needs of your people and your Sunday schedule of worship services.

8. A few ministers announce the entire year's program of sermons, including series of sermons, in advance and have the subjects printed so people can have a preview of the full year's preaching. I much prefer to announce a series at a time, thus maintaining freshness and newness in approach and appeal.

9. In preaching the series, stay with the plan which you have announced. Perhaps a series appears to lack enthusiasm. Do not just stop the series because you feel a bit discouraged. The immediate response of your people does not always tell the full story. If you have planned well, carry out your plan by preaching the full series according to your announcement.

10. Preaching a series of sermons with attractive subjects is like serving pumpkin pie with whipped cream. You know that in a cafeteria those cuts of pie with a touch of whipped cream will be taken first for the sake of appearance and perhaps taste. So the minister in preparing and presenting his series of sermons should seek to make every part of the plan interesting and attractive. But this should be done without

neglecting in the least the spiritual and Biblical ingredients that are part of good Biblical preaching. Often ministers fail at this very point, thinking that an attractive title or a psychologically planned series will carry the weight of good preaching. These points, though essential, are related to but not a substitute for good Biblical homiletics. These are discussed in the next chapter to make sure the basis of serial preaching is understood and practiced.

11. The length of series varies with different ministers and different congregations. Some prefer very short series, others enjoy extended series. When I came to my second congregation, they were unfamiliar with and surprised at my serial preaching, but they became so interested that my series were usually ten to thirteen sermons in length. Some prefer short series which can be completed in one month. Most months give opportunity for four evening or morning sermons while some have five Sundays. The series suggested in this book were intended to cover the interest of both those who favor short and long series. Surplus topics are suggested even in the month plan so that any one can make selections and not necessarily take all the suggestions.

12. Filing is very important in the preparation and development of series of sermons. A minister should always have a pad of paper or index cards on hand so that he can jot down texts for general preaching and texts for series of sermons. Such series suggestions should be posted in the file under section "Possible Series." These can be posted on 4 x 6 in. cards, 3 x 5 in. cards, manila folders, or cards one-half the size of a manila folder.

The minister should occasionally scan the series he has gleaned. He should keep them in mind and make additions as they develop in his thinking. This may appear to be a laborious plan, yet it is far easier than one thinks who has never tried it. Remember, the series suggestions are your own and therefore, they continue to be a part of you. Allow such possible series to steep and they will develop both in your thinking and on paper. You will discover that your mind will be increasingly alert for new and additional suggestions for serial preaching. All of this is in the background of your mind, the general reading of books, the study of the Bible and theology as well as your concordance reference study will funnel material into your file for series preaching. The plan will not work the same for all and some will find it more difficult than others. However, once you develop the homiletical habit you will be happily surprised, pleasantly pleased, and wonderfully rewarded.

13. The planning of a full year's program of preaching is very important to serial preaching.

First of all, when you plan for the coming weeks, months, or the entire year, you should make sure of the Scripture lesson and passages which will be stressed in the forthcoming Sunday School lessons. You should also take note of the special days, holy days, and holidays which you plan to observe. The arrangement of the series you select from the file for the period of time for which you are making your plan, should tie in with but not duplicate the material of the Sunday School lessons and the special day worship message. You will do well to place your plan of series on your desk with a card for each Sunday School lesson, each morning worship service message, and a card for the evening service at which time usually series of sermons are preached. When your selection has been made, allow the plan to steep and develop for two or three weeks. My own practice was to set up the program during the months of June and July before the August vacation so that when I left for vacation the entire year's program for morning and evening services was in readiness (on cards without lines, attached to envelopes) for the year of activity from the first Sunday in September through the last Sunday of the month of July.

As one sets up the program like this for a shorter period of time or for an entire year, and has these cards attached to envelopes or manila folders, one can then add any suggestions for the individual sermons on the cards or place such with clippings and references in the envelope or manila folder. Not all ministers may be able to make the plan for the year, or are even interested in doing so, but if you make a plan and carry it out in this manner you will find that preaching will be a sheer joy for both you and your people. You will discover that you will have a wealth of material constantly bubbling over through your mind and life. You will file this away for use in the days and months that lie ahead. Never again will you be at a loss for "a suitable text for next Sunday's sermon."

14. The goal for serial planning and preaching is very clear and simple. It is the very same goal as for all preaching: to build people spiritually with Biblical instruction.

a. In planning your serial preaching you should constantly evaluate the life of your congregation to determine and acquaint yourself with their points of strength and weakness. You should direct your planning to the specific needs of your flock. There will be a difference in serial preaching for the rural and city churches. There will be a difference of need and interest if your church is a mission organization or a traditionally established group of people. You should always keep in mind the particular times in which we are living, such as prosperity or adversity, war and peace, public calamity and general blessing. You should take into consideration the seasons of the year, and the special days according to the particular interest of the people. This program of general preaching should be planned in such a way that you can make substitutes when emergencies arise. It is, however, best to make the plan and follow it carefully.

This kind of general preaching will help to build your people in the way of instruction and inspiration. It will give them a new interest in the Bible and its study. It will give them a balanced diet for spiritual growth and they will come to a new appreciation of your careful planning for their spiritual blessings.

b. As series preaching will help your people, so it will be a blessing to you as a minister. It will set before you a goal and bring you a rich blessing. It will give you balance and variety in your preaching. It will avoid the riding of hobbies and allow your sermons both serial and otherwise to steep, grow and develop. It will save you time and effort. It will help you see more clearly and consistently the purpose and direction of the ministry. Your preaching program will lead up to certain points of interest and response at planned times in the year of activity and the lives of your people. It will give you the hope and the joy which results from careful long-range planning, thinking, reading, and study. It will save you many pitfalls and bring into focus much usable material from the life of your people, and from your own experience.

B. Biblical Homiletics in Sermon Construction

The underlying rules of Biblical homiletics in sermon construction are important. The following fundamental rules are laid down and are employed in the series suggested and in the special suggestions for special type series.

Every minister has his own personality and particular aptitudes and all may not agree with the detailed suggestions about to be given. Adaptation according to individual interest and aptitude is always possible. The following suggestions will be helpful toward understanding the pattern of this book and the real possibilities in Biblical preaching.

1. Use a text that has a unit or core of spiritual truth. The Bible is wonderfully constituted to furnish texts and passages of great spiritual value for salvation and the Christian way of life.

2. Read the text carefully in the light of its context in the chapter and book of the Bible. This is the secret to its understanding and will give you the key to its real meaning.

3. Study the text in the original language in which it was written. Consult the various translations of the text, both traditional and modern. The text patterns used in this volume are from the King James version because this is the most common pulpit Bible translation used and the most favored by the common people. Other translations are of real value and importance in arriving at the meaning of the text.

4. Divide the text into divisions, preparing:

a. A logical statement or simple declarative sentence which expresses the thought of the division.

b. A rhetorical statement of a word or two used as a key for memorization and presentation.

c. The quotation from the text in each division which forms the basis of the division.

d. Sub-divisions under each division can be made in the same manner as the divisions explained under a.

5. To prepare a theme of the entire message, make a simple declarative sentence which is a summary statement of the several divisions. Some ministers prefer to make the theme before the divisions but there is the ever present danger of inserting personal ideas outside the text if one uses this method. It is sounder procedure and much easier to make the

divisions first and then prepare a theme in the form of a declarative sentence as of a summary statement of these component parts.

6. At the top of the message, both in preparation and in its final form, indicate the purpose of the message with respect to explanation; topical or textual exposition; and with respect to content – ethical, doctrinal, exhortation, edificatory and instrumental.

7. Prepare the introduction, which may be: contextual, life content, pastoral contact, incident or illustration, or simple exhortation. The opening statement or attack is very important.

8. Prepare the conclusion, which may be: a summary of the message, its application to individuals, a covering illustration, or a pressing for decision.

9. Prepare a title of two or three words which describes the message and is spiritually attractive in the bulletin.

10. Prepare this complete outline on a card long before you preach it, attach it to the folder or envelope and allow it to "steep."

11. When Tuesday comes of the week you are to complete the sermon for Sunday, spread this outline over five or six large 8 1/2 by 11 inch pages filling in as much as possible under the sub-divisions and leaving open spaces under each sub-division for additional ideas.

12. Next consult commentaries, read other sermons in your study library on the subject or text, see encyclopedias, and works of theology on the doctrine or subject being considered. Fill in the open spaces as much as you can.

13. Leave this outline rest and steep until Thursday, and it will grow in your mind and mature. When Thursday comes, complete the outline, changing the order of collected statements if necessary, and type out a carefully studied outline or complete it in manuscript form. This will represent your logical, Biblical thinking on the text. After this long time consideration and careful preparation it will be easy to memorize and present on Sunday.

14. The importance of prayer in preparing Biblical sermons cannot be overstated or overemphasized. Careful study and thorough scholarship are indeed important for good sermon construction. Of basic importance for preaching are

the guidance of the Holy Spirit and the blessings of God. One should constantly pray the Lord to guide and sustain his effort in the study of the Word and in the making of Biblical sermons.

15. The preceding fourteen suggestions have given strength and emphasis to simple, Biblical-textual homiletics. It is true, this is not the only way of preaching. There are, for instance, those who prefer the topical method, using the text only as a spring-board from which to jump, never to come back to it until the following Sunday. This author is convinced that a topical sermon must also rest solidly on the Word of God if it is to be a blessing. One should not preach on topics which are not stated, implied, or inferred in the particular word or text under consideration. The pulpit of the Lord is the place for discussion of the Word of God, and not for ministerially conceived ideas or instructions which are not founded directly on the Word of God. The more closely the preacher adheres to the sure word of the Bible in the preparation of his sermons, whether textual or topical, the surer he will be about the presentation of God's truth, to interest his people and to build spiritually both his own life and those who hear him.

In the series suggestions in the chapter which follows, these conceptions and convictions are applied. They will be specifically listed in chapters three through seven. They are also carried out in chapters eight through eleven, even though the general emphasis in those suggested series refer to events. These ideas also find wider application in chapter twelve through sixteen. In these chapters the range of illustration comes from wider interest and sources. Yet the emphasis maintained in this book is a strong insistence on the use and blessing of the word of God. The reason for this is that God has blessed and will continue to bless not the words of man, but his own precious Word, the Holy Scriptures. This is His solemn promise and our comfort and inspiration, according to God's own statement, "For as the rain cometh down, and the snow from heaven, and returneth not thither, but watereth the earth, and maketh it bring forth and bud, that it may give seed to the sower, and bread to the eater: So shall my word be that goeth forth out of my mouth: it shall not return unto me void, but shall accomplish that which I please, and it shall prosper in the thing whereto I sent it" (Isaiah 55: 10, 11).

Chapter I
WORD CONNECTED SERIES

The most common type of serial preaching and often the easiest to prepare is the type that rests its strength on the connecting text word which is similar in each subject yet introduces variety into the total series. In this case particularly, variety of emphasis is important or the series becomes merely a repetition of the same idea in the same words. The use of the same textual key word with different references and different relationships in the Scriptures can result in a remarkable series of sermons, but such usage can also lead to dull preaching and the danger of killing the serial idea both for the minister and his people.

Concordance study cultivates this idea of word connected series. Be on the constant lookout for original ideas in word relationships which you will discover in studying the Word faithfully. This kind of series must steep for a long time if you are to avoid repetition in preparation and presentation.

ALL THINGS NEW

1. A New Birth. John 3: 3-7, "Except a man be born again, he cannot see the kingdom of God."

2. A New Heart. Jer. 31: 33, "I will put my law in their inward parts, and write it in their hearts."

3. A New Song. Ps. 40: 3, "And he hath put a new song in my mouth."

4. A New Command. John 13: 34, "A new commandment I give unto you, That ye love one another."

5. A New Destination. John 14: 1-3, "I go to prepare a place for you."

FRIENDSHIP OF FAITH

1. A True Friendship. I Sam. 18: 1-4, "The soul of Jonathan was knit with the soul of David."

2. A Tested Friendship. Prov. 17: 17, "A friend loveth at all times."

3. A Trusted Friendship. John 15: 13, 14, "Greater love hath no man than this, that a man lay down his life for his friends."

4. A Triumphant Friendship. I John 3: 2, "But we know that, when he shall appear, we shall be like him."

OBSTACLES TO CHRISTIAN LIVING

1. Ignorance. II Tim. 3: 1-9, "Ever learning, and never able to come to the knowledge of the truth."

2. Prejudice. Luke 4: 23-32, "No prophet is accepted in his own country."

3. Personal Righteousness. Matt. 23: 13-32, "Woe unto you, scribes and Pharisees, hypocrites!"

4. Personal Desires. Acts 19: 23-41, "Our craft is in danger to be set at nought."

5. Unbelief. Rom. 11: 32, "For God hath concluded them all in unbelief, that he might have mercy upon all."

CHRISTLIKE CITIZENS

1. Obey Authorities. Titus 3: 1, 2, "Put them in mind to be subject to principalities and powers, to obey magistrates."

2. Live Peacefully. Rom. 14: 19, "Let us therefore follow after the things which make for peace."

3. Build Your City. Neh. 6: 1-3, "I am doing a great work, so that I cannot come down."

4. Fight Evil. Micah 7: 1-4, "The good man is perished out of the earth."

5. Live Your Religion. Luke 7: 1-10, "They besought him instantly, saying, That he was worthy for whom he should do this."

GOALS FOR CHRISTIANS

1. Strive. Matt. 7: 7-14, "Ask, and it shall be given you . . ."

2. Seek. Matt. 6: 33, "But seek ye first the kingdom of God."

3. Fight. I Cor. 9: 24-27, "So run, that ye may obtain."

4. Look. Heb. 12: 1, 2, "Looking unto Jesus, the author and finisher of our faith."

5. Watch. Matt. 26: 41, "Watch and pray."

PRAYING CHRISTIANS

1. Abiding in Christ. John 15: 7, "If ye abide in me, and my words abide in you, ye shall ask what ye will, and it shall be done unto you."

2. Ask Freely of Christ. John 16: 24, "Ask, and ye shall receive, that your joy may be full."

3. Anxious About Nothing. Phil. 4: 6, "Be careful for nothing . . ."

4. United Prayer. Acts 12: 12, "Many were gathered together praying."

WITNESSES ON THE WAY

1. Witnesses of Christ. Luke: 24: 18, "Cleopas answering said unto him, Art thou only a stranger in Jerusalem . . ."

2. Witnessing before Others. Matt. 5: 16, "Let your light so shine before men, that they may see your good works . . ."

3. Power of Witnessing. John 15: 16, "I have chosen you . . . that ye should go and bring forth fruit . . . that whatsoever ye shall ask of the Father in my name, he may give it you."

4. Witnesses in All the World. Acts 1: 8, "Ye shall be witnesses unto me . . . unto the uttermost parts of the earth."

BIBLICAL REVELATION

1. Revelation of God. I Cor. 2: 9, 10, "Eye hath not seen, nor ear heard . . . But God hath revealed them unto us by his spirit."

2. Revelation Unfolded. Heb. 1: 1, 2, "God . . . hath in these last days spoken unto us by his son."

3. Revelation in Christ. John 1: 16, 17, "Grace and truth came by Jesus Christ."

4. Revelation for Light. Ps. 119: 105, "Thy word is a lamp unto my feet, and a light unto my path."

5. Revelation for Profit. II Tim. 3: 16, 17, "All scripture is given by inspiration of God, and is profitable . . . "

BIBLE GARDENS

1. The Garden of Creation. Gen. 2: 8, "And the Lord God planted a garden eastward in Eden; and there he put the man whom he had formed."

2. The Garden of Execution. Esth. 7: 10, "So they hanged Haman on the gallows that he had prepared for Mordecai."

3. The Garden of Coveteousness. I Kings 21: 1-16, "And Ahab spake unto Naboth, saying, Give me thy vineyard."

4. The Garden of Sorrow. Matt. 26: 36, "Then cometh Jesus with them unto a place called Gethsemane."

5. The Garden of Perfection. Rev. 22: 1-5, "And he shewed me a pure river of water of life . . . "

WATCHWORDS OF FAITH

1. Come. Isa. 1: 18, "Come now, and let us reason together . . . " Isa. 55: 1, "Come ye, buy, and eat . . . " Matt. 11: 28, "Come unto me . . . "

2. Follow. John 8: 12, "He that followeth me shall not walk in darkness, but shall have the light of life."

3. Learn. Rom. 15: 4, "For whatsoever things were written aforetime were written for our learning."

4. Pray. Phil. 4: 6, "In every thing by prayer and supplication with thanksgiving let your requests be made known unto God."

5. Labor. I Cor. 15: 58, "Always abounding in the work of the Lord, forasmuch as ye know that your labour is not in vain in the Lord."

6. Love. I John 3: 18, "My little children, let us not love in word, neither in tongue; but in deed and in truth."

SPIRITUAL GROWTH

1. Growth in Him. Eph. 4: 15, "But speaking the truth in love, may grow up into him in all things."

2. Growth in Faith. II Thess. 1: 3, "We are bound to thank God always for you . . . because that your faith groweth exceedingly."

3. Growth in Grace. II Peter 3: 18, "But grow in grace, and in the knowledge of our Lord and Saviour Jesus Christ."

4. Growth in the World. Matt. 13: 30, "Let both grow together until the harvest."

CONTINUE TO CONSECRATE

1. Continue in Prayer. Luke 6: 12, "He went out into a mountain to pray, and continued all night in prayer."

2. Continue in Fellowship. Luke 22: 28, "Ye are they which have continued with me in my temptations."

3. Continue in the Word. John 8: 31, "Then said Jesus . . . If ye continue in my word, then are ye my disciples indeed."

4. Continue in Love. John 15: 9, "As the Father hath loved me, so have I loved you: continue ye in my love."

5. Continue in Grace. Acts 13: 43, "Paul and Barnabas . . . persuaded them to continue in the grace of God."

CONSIDER GODLY LIVING

1. Consider God. Ps. 50: 22, "Now consider this, ye that forget God, lest I tear you in pieces, and there be none to deliver."

2. Consider the Poor. Ps. 41: 1, "Blessed is he that considereth the poor."

3. Consider Adversity. Eccl. 7: 14, "In the day of adversity consider."

4. Consider your Ways. Hag. 1: 5, 7, "Thus saith the Lord of hosts; Consider your ways."

5. Consider Christ. Heb. 3: 1, "Wherefore, holy brethren, partakers of the heavenly calling, consider the Apostle and High Priest of our profession, Christ Jesus."

THE CHRISTIAN CONSCIENCE

1. A Good Conscience. I Peter 3: 16, "Having a good conscience; that . . . they may be ashamed that falsely accuse your good conversation in Christ."

2. A Pure Conscience. I Tim. 3: 9, "Holding the mystery of the faith in a pure conscience."

3. A Respected Conscience. Rom. 14: 21, "It is good neither to eat flesh . . . nor anything whereby thy brother stumbleth, or is offended . . ."

4. A Cleansed Conscience. Heb. 9: 14, "How much more shall the blood of Christ . . . purge your conscience from dead works to serve the living God."

5. A Witnessing Conscience. Rom. 2: 15, "Which shew the work of the law written in their hearts, their conscience also bearing witness."

HOPE FOR THE HELPLESS

1. Saved by Hope. Rom. 8: 24, "For we are saved by hope."

2. Anchored by Hope. Heb. 6: 19, "Which hope we have as an anchor of the soul, both sure and stedfast.

3. Comforted by Hope. John 14: 18, "I will not leave you comfortless."

4. Encouraged by Hope. Ps. 31: 24, "Be of good courage, and he shall strengthen your heart, all ye that hope in the Lord."

5. Continued by Hope. Ps. 71: 14, "But I will hope continually."

GOD'S BLESSED WORK

1. God's Work Completed. Gen. 2: 2, "And on the seventh day God ended his work which he had made."

2. God's Work Recognized. Neh. 6: 16, " . . . for they perceived that this work was wrought of our God."

3. God's Work Established. Ps. 90: 17, "Establish thou the work of our hands upon us; yea, the work of our hands establish thou it."

CONSECRATED WORK

1. Accepted Work. Eccl. 9: 7, "Go thy way, eat thy bread with joy . . . for God now accepteth thy works."

2. Applied Work. Eccl. 8: 9, "All this have I seen, and applied my heart unto every work that is done under the sun."

3. Applauded Work. Matt. 23: 5, "But all their works they do for to be seen of men."

4. Appraised Work. Eccl. 12: 14, "For God shall bring every work into judgment . . . whether it be good, or whether it be evil."

THE WORD OF GOD

1. Proceeded Word. Deut. 8: 3, "Man doth not live by bread only, but by every word that proceedeth out of the mouth of the Lord . . . "

2. Powerful Word. Heb. 11: 3, "Through faith we understand that the worlds were framed by the word of God."

3. Perceptable Word. Isa. 30: 21, "And thine ears shall hear a word behind thee, saying, This is the way, walk ye in it."

4. Permanent Word. Matt. 24: 35, "Heaven and earth shall pass away, but my words shall not pass away."

THE WORD OF MEN

1. The Acceptable Word. Ps. 19: 4, "Their line is gone out through all the earth, and their words to the end of the world."

2. A Seasonable Word. Prov. 15: 23, "A word spoken in due season, how good is it."

3. Idle Words. Matt. 12: 36, " . . . every idle word that men shall speak, they shall give account thereof in the day of judgment."

4. Sowing the Word. Mark 4: 14, "The sower soweth the word."

LIVING BY THE WORD

1. Holding Forth the Word. Phil. 2: 16, "Holding forth the word of life."

2. Nourished in the Word. I Tim. 4: 6, " . . . a good minister of Jesus Christ, nourished up in the words of faith and of good doctrine."

3. Doers of the Word. James 1: 22, "But be ye doers of the word, and not hearers only."

4. Manifest the Word. Titus 1: 3, "But hath in due times manifested his word through preaching, which is committed unto me . . . "

5. Comfort from the Word. I Thess. 4: 18, "Wherefore comfort one another with these words."

KINDS OF LIFE

1. Physical Life. Gen. 2: 7, "And the Lord God . . . breathed into his nostrils the breath of life."

2. Spiritual Life. Rom. 6: 4, "That like as Christ was raised . . . even so we also should walk in newness of life."

3. Eternal Life. John 17: 3, "And this is life eternal, that they might know thee the only true God, and Jesus Christ, whom thou hast sent."

THE NECESSITY OF LIGHT

1. The Lord our Light. Ps. 27: 1, "The Lord is my light and my salvation."

2. Light for the Pathway. Ps. 119: 105, "Thy word is a lamp unto my feet, and a light unto my path."

3. Light for Faith. John 12: 36, "While ye have light, believe in the light."

4. Light for Witnessing. Matt. 5: 16, "Let your light so shine before men, that they may see your good works, and glorify your Father. . ."

5. Light for the World. John 8: 12, "Then spake Jesus again unto them, saying, I am the light of the world."

QUESTS OF LIFE

1. Looking for Light. Ps. 34: 5, "They looked unto him, and were lightened."

2. Looking for Salvation. Isa. 45: 22, "Look unto me, and be ye saved, all ends of the earth."

3. Looking for Peace. Jer. 8: 15, "We looked for peace, but no good came."

4. Looking for the Blessed Hope. Titus 2: 13, "Looking for that blessed hope, and the glorious appearing of the great God . . ."

5. Looking for a City. Heb. 11: 10, "For he looked for a city which hath foundations, whose builder and maker is God."

THE ABUNDANT LIFE

1. Abounding in Fruit. Phil. 4: 17, "I desire fruit that may abound to your account."

2. Abounding in Grace. Rom. 5: 20, "But where sin abounded, grace did much more abound."

3. Abounding in Charity. II Thess. 1: 3, "The charity of every one of you all toward each other aboundeth."

4. Abounding in Hope. Rom. 15: 13, "That ye may abound in hope, through the power of the Holy Ghost."

5. Abounding in Service. I Cor. 15: 58, "Be ye stedfast, unmoveable, always abounding in the work of the Lord."

6. Abounding in Thanksgiving. Col. 2: 7, "Rooted and built up in him, and stablished in the faith . . . abounding therein with thanksgiving."

SINS OF THE SAINTS

1. Sin Condemned. II Sam. 12: 7, "Thou art the man."

2. Sin Confessed. Ps. 32: 5, "I acknowledged my sin unto thee."

3. Sin Covered. Ps. 32: 1, "Blessed is he whose . . . sin is covered."

4. Sin Cleansed. Isa. 1: 18, "Though your sins be as scarlet, they shall be as white as snow."

SECRETS TO REMEMBER

1. The Secret of the Lord. Ps. 25: 14, "The secret of the Lord is with them that fear him."

2. Secret Errors. Ps. 19: 12, "Cleanse thou me from secret faults."

3. The Secret Place of the Most High. Ps. 91: 1, "He that dwelleth in the secret place of the most High shall abide under the shadow of the Almighty."

4. Giving Alms in Secret. Matt. 6: 4, "That thine alms may be in secret . . . "

DOORS TO CONSIDER

1. The Door of Sin. Gen. 4: 7, "If thou doest not well, sin lieth at the door."

2. The Door of Fellowship. Job 31: 32, "I opened my doors to the traveller."

3. The Door of Life. John 10: 9, "I am the door: by me if any man enter in, he shall be saved."

4. The Door of Opportunity. I Cor. 16: 9, "For a great door and effectual is opened unto me."

5. The Door of Salvation. Rev. 3: 20, "Behold, I stand at the door, and knock."

6. The Door of Heaven. Ps. 78: 23, "Though he had . . . opened the doors of heaven."

PRECIOUS POSSESSIONS

1. Precious Word. I Sam. 3: 1, "And the word of the Lord was precious in those days."

2. Precious Soul. I Sam. 26: 21, "My soul was precious in thine eyes this day."

3. Precious Redemption. Ps. 49: 8, "For the redemption of their soul is precious."

4. Precious Corner Stone. I Peter 2: 6, "I lay in Sion a chief corner stone."

5. Precious Blood. I Peter 1: 19, "But with the precious blood of Christ."

6. Precious Faith. II Peter 1: 1, "Simon Peter, . . . to them that have obtained like precious faith with us."

7. Precious Promises. II Peter 1: 4, "Whereby are given unto us exceeding great and precious promises."

LIFE IN THE WORD

1. Born Again by the Word. I Peter 1: 23, "Being born again, . . . by the word of God."

2. Sincere Milk of the Word. I Peter 2: 2, "Desire the sincere milk of the word."

3. Obey the Word. I Peter 3: 1, "That, if any obey not the word, they also may without the word be won . . ."

4. Keep the Word. I John 2: 5, "But whoso keepeth his word, in him verily is the love of God perfected."

CERTIFIED CERTAINTIES

1. I Know God's Help. Ps. 56: 9, "When I cry unto thee, then shall my enemies turn back: this I know; for God is for me."

2. I Know My Redeemer Liveth. Job 19: 25, "For I know that my redeemer liveth."

3. I Know the Love of Christ. Eph. 3: 19, "And to know the love of Christ, which passeth knowledge."

4. I Know God's Providence. Rom. 8: 28, "And we know that all things work together for good to them that love God."

5. I Know of My House Eternal. II Cor. 5: 1, "For we know that if our earthly house of this tabernacle were dissolved, we have a building of God . . ."

THE NECESSITY OF GRACE

1. Grace for Salvation. Eph. 2: 8, "For by grace are ye saved through faith."

2. Grace for Instruction. Titus 2: 11, 12, "For the grace of God . . . hath appeared . . . teaching us . . ."

3. Grace for Growth. II Peter 3: 18, "But grow in grace."

4. Grace for Justification. Rom. 3: 24, "Being justified freely by his grace."

5. Grace for Witnessing. Col. 4: 6, "Let your speech be alway with grace . . ."

6. Grace for Heart Establishment. Heb. 13: 9, "For it is a good thing that the heart be established with grace."

WHAT IS LIFE?

1. Life Is Created by God. Gen. 1: 26, "And God said, Let us make man . . . "

2. Life Needs Guidance. Ps. 16: 11, "Thou wilt shew me the path of life."

3. Life Requires Trust. Matt. 6: 25, "Take no thought for your life . . . "

4. Life Is More Than Meat. Luke 12: 23, "The life is more than meat."

5. Life Is Hid in God. Col. 3: 3, "Your life is hid with Christ in God."

SPIRITUAL FOUNDATIONS

1. A Foundation Laid. Isa. 28: 16, "Behold, I lay in Zion for a foundation a stone, a tried stone, a precious corner stone, a sure foundation."

2. A Foundation Secured. Luke 6: 48, "He is like a man which built an house, and digged deep, and laid the foundation on a rock."

3. A Foundation Built. I Cor. 3: 11, 12, "For other foundation can no man lay than that is laid, which is Jesus Christ."

4. A Foundation Expected. Heb. 11: 10, "For he looked for a city which hath foundations."

SUSTAINED BY CHRIST

1. Christ's Strength. Phil. 4: 13, "I can do all things through Christ which strengtheneth me."

2. Christ's Grace. II Cor. 12: 9, "And he said unto me, My grace is sufficient for thee."

3. Christ's Providence. Rom. 8: 28, "And we know that all things work together for good to them that love God."

4. Christ's Redemption. II Tim. 1: 12, "For I know whom I have believed, and am persuaded that he is able to keep that which I have committed unto him against that day."

5. Christ's Presence. Matt. 28: 19, 20, "Lo, I am with you alway."

SPIRITUAL GIVING

1. Cheerful Giving. II Cor. 9: 7, "God loveth a cheerful giver."

2. Systematic Giving. I Cor. 16: 2, "Upon the first day of the week let every one of you lay by him in store, as God hath prospered him."

3. Personal Giving. Luke 6: 38, "Give, and it shall be given unto you . . ."

4. Devoted Giving. Luke 18: 22-25, "Jesus . . . said unto him, Yet lackest thou one thing: sell all that thou hast, and distribute unto the poor."

STEWARDSHIP OF LIFE

1. Chosen Stewards. John 15: 16, "I have chosen you . . . that whatsoever ye shall ask of the Father in my name, he may give it you."

2. Consecrated Stewards. I Tim. 4: 14, 15, "Neglect not the gift that is in thee, which was given thee by the prophecy, with the laying on of the hands."

3. Convinced Steward. John 14: 12, "He that believeth on me, the works that I do shall he do also, and greater works than these shall he do."

4. Co-operating Stewards. I Cor. 3: 9, "For we are labourers together with God."

DELIVERANCE REALITIES

1. God's Promise to Deliver. Jer. 1: 8, "I am with thee to deliver thee."

2. God's Ability to Deliver. Dan. 3: 17, "Our God whom we serve is able to deliver us . . . "

3. Deliverance from Evil. Matt. 6: 13, "Deliver us from evil."

4. Delivered for our Offences. Rom. 4: 25, "Who was delivered for our offences."

5. A Delivered Faith. Jude 3, " . . . the faith which was once delivered unto the saints."

HEART EXPERIENCES

1. Heart Love. Matt. 22: 37, "Thou shalt love the Lord thy God with all thy heart."

2. Heart Examination. I Sam. 16: 7, " . . . but the Lord looketh on the heart."

3. Heart Music. Job 29: 13, ". . . and I caused the widow's heart to sing for joy."

4. Heart Certainty. Ps. 108: 1, "O God, my heart is fixed . . . ."

5. Heart Treasury. Ps. 119: 11, "Thy word have I hid in mine heart."

6. Heart Bitterness. Prov. 14: 10, "The heart knoweth his own bitterness."

7. Heart Sanctification. I Peter 3: 15, "But sanctify the Lord God in your hearts."

SIGNS OF THE LORD

1. A Requested Sign. Isa. 7: 11, "Ask thee a sign of the Lord thy God."

2. An Everlasting Sign. Isa. 55: 13, " . . . and it shall be to the Lord for a name, for an everlasting sign that shall not be cut off."

3. A Placed Sign. Ezek. 12: 6, "I have set thee for a sign unto the house of Israel."

4. A Sign Spoken Against. Luke 2: 34, "Behold, this child is set . . . for a sign which shall be spoken against."

5. Approving Signs. Acts 2: 22, "Jesus of Nazareth, a man approved of God among you by miracles and wonders and signs."

ACCEPTABLE RELIGION

1. Acceptable to God. Ps. 19: 14, "Let the words of my mouth, and the meditation of my heart, be acceptable in thy sight, O Lord."

2. Acceptable to the Brethren. Deut. 33: 24, "Let Asher... be acceptable to his brethren."

3. Acceptable Time. II Cor. 6: 2, "Behold, now is the accepted time . . ."

4. Acceptable Supplication. Jer. 42: 2, "Let . . . our supplication be accepted."

5. Acceptable in Christ. Eph. 1: 6, " . . . wherein he hath made us accepted in the beloved."

ABUNDANT LIVING

1. Abundant Provision. I Chron. 22: 3, "And David prepared . . . in abundance."

2. Abundant Grace. Rom. 5: 17, " . . . much more they which receive abundance of grace . . . shall reign in life by one, Jesus Christ."

3. Abundant Possessions. Luke 21: 4, "For all these have of their abundance cast in unto the offerings of God: but she of her penury."

4. Abundant Blessings. Eph. 3: 20, "Now unto him that is able to do exceeding abundantly above all that we ask or think."

5. Abundant Labor. II Cor. 1: 12, "We have had our conversation in the world, and more abundantly to you-ward."

PRECIOUS POSSIBILITIES

1. Precious Wisdom. Prov. 3: 15, "She is more precious than rubies: and all the things thou canst desire are not to be compared unto her."

2. Precious Name. Eccles. 7: 1, "A good name is better than precious ointment."

3. Precious Cornerstone. I Peter 2: 6, "Behold I lay in Sion a chief cornerstone, elect, precious: and he that believeth on him shall not be confounded."

4. Precious Trial. I Peter 1: 7, "That the trial of your faith, being much more precious than of gold that perisheth."

5. Precious Saviour. I Peter 2: 7, "Unto you therefore which believe he is precious."

6. Precious Promises. II Peter 1: 4, "Whereby are given unto us exceeding great and precious promises."

BIBLE GREATS

1. A Great Nation. Gen. 12: 2, "And I will make of thee a great nation, and I will bless thee, and make thy name great."

2. A Great House. II Chron. 2: 5, "And the house which I build is great: for great is our God above all gods."

3. A Great Work. Neh. 6: 3, "I am doing a great work, so that I cannot come down."

4. A Great Ransom. Job 36: 18, "Beware lest he take thee away with his stroke: then a great ransom cannot deliver thee."

5. A Great Reward. Matt. 5: 12, "Great is your reward in heaven: for so persecuted they the prophets which were before you."

6. A Great Faith. Matt. 15: 28, "O woman, great is thy faith: be it unto thee even as thou wilt."

7. A Great Commandment. Matt. 22: 36, "Master, which is the great commandment in the law?"

8. A Great Mystery. I Tim. 3: 16, "And without controversy great is the mystery of godliness."

9. A Great Salvation. Heb. 2: 3, "How shall we escape, if we neglect so great a salvation?"

WAITING FOR BLESSINGS

1. Waiting for Salvation. Gen. 49: 18, "I have waited for thy salvation, O Lord."

2. Waiting for God. Ps. 62: 5, "My soul, wait thou only upon God; for my expectation is from him."

3. Waiting for Strength. Isa. 40: 31, "They that wait upon the Lord shall renew their strength."

4. Waiting for Vision. Hab. 2: 3, "For the vision is yet for an appointed time, but at the end it shall speak . . . though it tarry, wait for it."

5. Waiting for Promise. Acts 1: 4, "But wait for the promise of the Father, which, saith he, ye have heard of me."

6. Waiting for Adoption. Rom. 8: 33, "Who shall lay any thing to the charge of God's elect? It is God that justifieth."

7. Waiting for Hope. Gal. 5: 5, "For we through the Spirit wait for the hope of righteousness by faith."

8. Waiting for Christ. I Thess. 1: 10, "And to wait for his Son from heaven, whom he raised from the dead, even Jesus."

GRIEVOUS EXPERIENCES

1. A Grievous Warning. Gen. 21: 11, "And the thing was very grievous in Abraham's sight because of his son."

2. A Grievous Anger. Prov. 15: 1, "A soft answer turneth away wrath: but grievous words stir up anger."

3. A Grievous Wound. Jer. 30: 12, "For thus saith the Lord, Thy bruise is incurable, and thy wound is grievous."

4. A Grievous Burden. Matt. 23: 4, "For they bind heavy burdens and grievous to be borne."

5. A Grievous Chastening. Heb. 12: 11, "Now no chastening for the present seemeth to be joyous, but grievous."

GREATER COMPARISONS

1. A Greater House. Hag. 2: 9, "The glory of this latter house shall be greater than of the former, saith the Lord of hosts."
2. A Greater Temple. Matt. 12: 6, "But I say unto you, That in this place is one greater than the temple."
3. A Greater Manifestation. John 1: 50, "Thou shalt see greater things than these."
4. A Greater God. John 10: 29, "My Father, which gave them me, is greater than all."
5. A Greater Love. John 15: 13, "Greater love hath no man than this, that a man lay down his life for his friends."

PLACES OF BLESSING

1. A Holy Place. Ex. 3: 5, "Put off thy shoes from off thy feet, for the place whereon thou standest is holy ground."
2. A Satisfying Place. Judg. 18: 10, "A place where there is no want of anything that is in the earth."
3. A Straight Place. Isa. 49: 20, "The place is too strait for me: give place to me that I may dwell."
4. A Hiding Place. Ps. 32: 7, "Thou art my hiding place; thou shalt preserve me from trouble."
5. A Dwelling Place. Ps. 90: 1, "Lord, thou hast been our dwelling place in all generations."
6. An Idolatrous Place. I Kings 11: 7, "Then did Solomon build an high place for Chemosh, the abomination of Moab."

Chapter II

IDEA CONNECTED SERIES

Closely allied to the word connected series is the idea of connected series. Some would call these topical series, and would use them merely as topics without a fundamental Biblical textual exposition to give the message secure footing. Those who would be tempted to proceed thus should reread the Introduction.

As in the Word connected series the actual word employed is repeated in each subject, so in idea connected series the same idea occurs in each subject but with a variety of emphasis and treating new phase of the general subject of the entire series. There is danger in this kind of serial preaching lest the preacher repeat himself often. There must be a connection, but only to the extent that each sermon becomes a separate link in the total chain of the series. The links are held together by the one central idea of the series but each sermon of such a series reflects a different light and information for the interest and the instruction of the listener.

Sometimes word connected series and idea connected series overlap. Some ministers have some sub-subjects in the series with identical word connections and others with only the idea connecting them. If such a combination makes a good series, well and good; however it is better to separate the two types of serial preaching for the listening pleasure of your people.

Some people criticize this type of series, claiming that it takes the minister too far from the Word. Indeed the opposite is true if he preaches correctly because this type of series is based on the textual exposition of each sub-topic, the connection being based only on the fundamental idea pervading the series as a whole.

POWERFUL PRESENCE

1. Presence of Leadership. Ex. 33: 15, "And he said unto him, If thy presence go not with me, carry us not up hence."

2. Presence of Judgment. Job 23: 15, "Therefore am I troubled at his presence: when I consider, I am afraid of him."

3. Presence of Joy. Ps. 16: 11, "Thou wilt shew me the path of life: in thy presence is fulness of joy."

4. Presence of Refreshing. Acts 3: 19, "Repent ye therefore, ... when the times of refreshing shall come from the presence of the Lord."

5. Presence of an Angel. Isa. 63: 9, "In all their affliction he was afflicted, and the angel of his presence saved them."

IMPORTANT NEGATIVES

1. Fear Not. Isa. 43: 1, "O Israel, Fear not: for I have redeemed thee, I have called thee by thy name; thou art mine."

2. Fret Not. Ps. 37: 1, "Fret not thyself because of evil-doers, neither be thou envious against the workers of iniquity."

3. Forget Not. Ps. 103: 2, "Bless the Lord, O my soul, and forget not all his benefits."

4. Lay Not Up Treasures. Matt. 6: 19, "Lay not up for yourselves treasures upon earth, where moth and rust doth corrupt."

5. Resist Not. Matt. 5: 39, "But I say unto you, That ye resist not evil."

BE OF BLESSING

1. Be of Good Courage. Ps. 31: 24, "Be of good courage, and he shall strengthen your heart, all ye that hope in the Lord."

2. Be Kind. Eph. 4: 32, "And be ye kind one to another, tenderhearted, forgiving one another."

3. Be Perfect. Matt. 5: 48, "Be ye therefore perfect, even as your Father which is in heaven is perfect."

4. Be Ready. Matt. 24: 44, "Therefore be ye also ready: for in such an hour as ye think not the Son of man cometh."

5. Be Doers. James 1: 22, "But be ye doers of the word, and not hearers only, deceiving your own selves."

6. Be Faithful. Rev. 2: 10, "Be thou faithful unto death, and I will give thee a crown of life."

COMPLETE COMFORT

1. Comfort of the Scriptures. Rom. 15: 4, "That we through patience and comfort of the scriptures might have hope."

2. Comfort of the Holy Ghost. Acts 9: 31, "And in the comfort of the Holy Ghost were multiplied."

3. Comfort in One Another. II Cor. 7: 13, "Therefore we were comforted in your comfort."

4. Comfort as of a Mother. Isa. 66: 13, "As one whom his mother comforteth, so will I comfort you."

5. Comfort for Eternity. Luke 16: 25, "But now he is comforted, and thou art tormented."

THE CHURCH FAMILY

1. A Fellowship. Acts 2: 42, "And they continued stedfastly in the apostles' doctrine and fellowship."

2. A Brotherhood. I Peter 2: 17, "Honour all men. Love the brotherhood."

3. Unity in Diversity. I Cor. 12: 4, "Now there are diversities of gifts, but the same Spirit."

4. Weak and Strong. Rom. 15: 1, "We then that are strong ought to bear the infirmities of the weak."

5. Children Also. Matt. 19: 13, "Then were there brought unto him little children, that he should put his hands on them."

ASPECTS OF THE CHURCH

1. A Flock. I Peter 5: 2, "Feed the flock of God which is among you, taking the oversight thereof."

2. A Fellowship. I John 1: 3, "That ye also may have fellowship with us."

3. A Field. I Cor. 3: 9, "For we are labourers together with God: ye are God's husbandry."

4. A Family. Eph. 3: 15, "Of whom the whole family in heaven and earth is named."

5. A Future. John 10: 28, "And I give unto them eternal life; and they shall never perish."

RESPONSIBILITIES FOR THE CHURCH

1. Unity Desired. Acts 5: 12, "They were all with one accord in Solomon's porch."

2. Evangelism. Acts 1: 8, "And ye shall be witnesses unto me."

3. Missions. Matt. 28: 19, "Go ye therefore, and teach all nations, baptizing them in the name of the Father, and of the Son, and of the Holy Ghost."

4. Instruction. I Cor. 4: 17, "As I teach every where in every church."

5. Charity. II Cor. 8: 4, "Praying us with much intreaty that we should receive the gift."

LIFE IN THE CHURCH

1. A Life of Prayer. Acts 1: 14, "These all continued with one accord in prayer and supplication."

2. Pentecost for Life. Acts 2: 1, "And when the day of Pentecost was fully come, they were all with one accord in one place."

3. A Life of Praise. Acts 2: 47, "Praising God, and having favour with all the people."

4. A Life Preserved. Acts 4: 12, "For there is none other name under heaven given among men, whereby we must be saved."

THE PLAN OF THE CHURCH

1. The Church in the Wilderness. Acts 7: 38, "This is he, that was in the church in the wilderness."

2. The Church in the House. Rom. 16: 5, "Likewise greet the church that is in their house."

3. The Church in Christ. Eph. 5: 24, "As the church is subject unto Christ."

4. The Church in the Future. Acts 2: 47, "And the Lord added to the church daily such as should be saved."

5. The Church in Persecution. Acts 8: 3, "As for Saul, he made havock of the church."

PORTRAITS OF HUMANITY

1. The Sinner. Rom. 7: 14, "For we know that the law is spiritual: but I am carnal, sold under sin."

2. The Witness. Acts 1: 8, "And ye shall be witnesses unto me."

3. The Preacher. II Tim. 4: 2, "Preach the word."

4. The Church. Acts 2: 42, "They continued stedfastly in the apostles' doctrine and fellowship, and in breaking of bread, and in prayers."

5. The Saviour. John 14: 6, "Jesus saith unto him, I am the way, the truth, and the life."

SPIRITUAL TRAVELERS

1. Our Captain. Heb. 2: 10, "To make the captain of their salvation perfect through sufferings."

2. Storm at Sea. Matt. 8: 25, "And his disciples came to him, and awoke him, saying, Lord, save us: we perish."

3. Our Anchor. Heb. 6: 19, "Which hope we have as an anchor of the soul, both sure and stedfast."

4. The Steward. Luke 16: 2, "Give an account of thy stewardship; for thou mayest be no longer steward."

5. The Harbor Eternal. Rev. 21: 1, "And I saw a new heaven and a new earth."

GOALS FOR CHRISTIANS

1. Try the Spirits. I John 4: 1, "Beloved, believe not every spirit, but try the spirits whether they are of God."

2. Pray as a Church. Acts 1: 14, "These all continued with one accord in prayer and supplication."

3. Neglect Not Salvation. Heb. 2: 3, "How shall we escape, if we neglect so great salvation."

4. Trusting the Medication. I Tim. 3: 5, "For if a man know not how to rule his own house, how shall he take care of the church of God?"

5. Maintaining the Home. Prov. 11: 29, "He that troubleth his own house shall inherit the wind."

ATTAINMENTS FOR CHRISTIANS

1. Being a Missionary. Acts 8: 29, "Then the Spirit said unto Philip, Go near, and join thyself to this chariot."

2. Foster Spiritual Order. I Cor. 14: 40, "Let all things be done decently and in order."

3. Enjoy God's Day. Isa. 58: 13, "If thou turn away thy foot from the sabbath, from doing thy pleasure on my holy day."

4. Using Our Bibles. Ps. 119, 105, "Thy word is a lamp unto my feet, and a light unto my path."

5. Follow Christian Liberty. I Cor. 6: 12, "All things are lawful unto me, but all things are not expedient."

6. Prepare for Judgment. Eccl. 12: 14, "For God shall bring every work into judgment."

QUESTIONS WE ASK

1. Did the Whale Swallow Jonah? Jonah 1: 17, "Now the Lord had prepared a great fish to swallow up Jonah."

2. Is it Good to Suffer Affliction? Heb. 12: 11, "Nevertheless afterward it yieldeth the peaceable fruit of righteousness unto them which are exercised thereby."

3. Does Man Need to Convert Himself? Phil. 2: 13, "For it is God which worketh in you both to will and to do of his good pleasure."

4. Are the Wicked Prosperous? Job 21: 17, "How oft is the candle of the wicked put out! and how oft cometh their destruction upon them."

5. Is Life Fully Planned? Ps. 16: 5, "The Lord is the portion of mine inheritance and of my cup: thou maintainest my lot."

6. Where are the Dead? I Thess. 4: 13, "But I would not have you to be ignorant, brethren, concerning them which are asleep."

7. Why So Many Denominations? John 17: 21, "That they all may be one; as thou, Father, art in me, and I in thee, that they also may be one in us."

8. Which Observe, Sabbath or Sunday? Ex. 20: 8, "Remember the sabbath day, to keep it holy." Acts 20: 7, "And upon the first day of the week, when the disciples came together to break bread, Paul preached unto them."

9. When Will Jesus Return? Matt. 24: 44, "Therefore be ye also ready: for in such an hour as ye think not the Son of man cometh."

STRANGE TEXTS FOR A STRANGE TIME

1. A Short Bed. Isa. 28: 20, "For the bed is shorter than that a man can stretch himself on it: and the covering narrower than that he can wrap himself in it."

2. Jumping Over a Wall. II Sam. 22: 30, "By my God have I leaped over a wall."

3. The Christian Fool. I Cor. 4: 10, "We are fools for Christ's sake, but ye are wise in Christ."

4. Sharpening Iron. Prov. 27: 17. "Iron sharpeneth iron; so a man sharpeneth the countenance of his friend.

5. Bow at a Venture. I Kings 22: 34, "And a certain man drew a bow at a venture, and smote the king of Israel."

6. Keys of the Kingdom. Matt. 16: 19, "And I will give unto thee the keys of the kingdom of heaven."

7. An Unturned Cake. Hos. 7: 8, "Ephraim, he hath mixed himself among the people; Ephraim is a cake not turned."

8. Kissing the Son. Ps. 2: 12, "Kiss the Son, lest he be angry, and ye perish from the way."

SPIRITUAL MALADIES

1. Spiritual Anemia. Judg. 16: 20, "And he wist not that the Lord was departed from him."

2. Poor Wind. I Cor. 9: 24, "Know ye not that they which run in a race run all, but one receiveth the prize?"

3. Spiritual Deafness. Rev. 2: 7, "He that hath an ear, let him hear what the Spirit saith unto the churches."

4. Poor Diet. Isa. 55: 2, "Wherefore do ye spend money for that which is not bread? and your labour for that which satisfieth not?"

5. Tongue Tied. Luke 19: 40, "I tell you that, if these should hold their peace, the stones would immediately cry out."

6. Throbbing Headaches. Rom. 7: 25, "So then with the mind I myself serve the law of God; but with the flesh the law of sin."

7. A Weak Heart. Ps. 119: 80, "Let my heart be sound in thy statutes; that I be not ashamed."

8. Spiritual Blindness. Matt. 13: 11, "Because it is given unto you to know the mysteries of the kingdom of heaven, but to them it is not given."

BIBLE GARDENS

1. The Garden of Responsibility. Gen. 2: 15, "And the Lord God took the man, and put him into the garden of Eden to dress it and to keep it."

2. The Garden of Immorality. Esth. 1: 11, "To shew the people and the princes her beauty: for she was fair to look on."

3. The Garden of Jealousy. I Kings 21: 20, "And Ahab said to Elijah, Hast thou found me, O mine enemy?"

4. The Garden of Blessing. Rev. 22: 1, "And he shewed me a pure river of water of life, clear as crystal, proceeding out of the throne of God and of the Lamb."

QUESTIONS ABOUT THE HOME

1. Who is to Blame? Gen. 3: 4, "And the serpent said unto the woman, Ye shalt not surely die."

2. Inconsistent Parents. Josh. 24: 15, "But as for me and my house, we will serve the Lord."

3. Believing Wife; Unbelieving Husband. I Cor. 7: 14, "For the unbelieving husband is sanctified by the wife, and the unbelieving wife is sanctified by the husband."

4. Disobedient Children. Ex. 20: 12, "Honour thy father and thy mother: that thy days may be long upon the land which the Lord thy God giveth thee."

5. The Problem Mother-in-Law. Ruth 1: 16, "And Ruth said, Intreat me not to leave thee, or to return from following after thee."

6. The Open Casket. Gen. 35: 19, "And Rachel died, and was buried in the way to Ephrath, which is Bethlehem."

7. Second Marriage. Matt. 22: 30, "For in the resurrection they neither marry, nor are given in marriage."

8. Scriptural Divorce. Matt. 5: 32, "Whosoever shall put away his wife, saving for the cause of fornication, causeth her to commit adultery."

THE CYCLE OF LIFE

1. Newborn Babes. I Peter 2: 2, "As newborn babes, desire the sincere milk of the word, that ye may grow thereby."

2. Childlike Humility. Matt. 19: 14, "Suffer little children, and forbid them not, to come unto me: for of such is the kingdom of heaven."

3. Days of Youth. Eccl. 12: 1, "Remember now thy Creator in the days of thy youth."

4. Parental Advice. Eph. 6: 4, "And, ye fathers, provoke not your children to wrath."

5. Old Age. Ps. 71: 18, "Now also when I am old and greyheaded, O God, forsake me not."

6. Heavenly Maturity. II Cor. 5: 1, "We have a building of God, an house not made with hands, eternal in the heavens."

MESSAGES FROM GOD

1. To Parents. Prov. 22: 6, "Train up a child in the way he should go: and when he is old, he will not depart from it."

2. To Young People. Prov. 1: 10, "My son, if sinners entice thee, consent thou not."

3. To Sinners. Ezek. 18: 32, "For I have no pleasure in the death of him that dieth, saith the Lord God."

4. To Saints. II Cor. 10: 4, "For the weapons of our warfare are not carnal, but mighty through God."

5. To God's Workers. Isa. 55: 11, "So shall my word be that goeth forth out of my mouth: it shall not return unto me void."

LIFE'S CHALLENGES

1. The Devil's Challenge. Gen. 3: 9, "And the Lord God called unto Adam, and said unto him, Where art thou?"

2. A Lawyer's Challenge. Acts 26: 28, "Then Agrippa said unto Paul, Almost thou persuadest me to be a Christian."

3. A Preacher's Challenge. Acts 2: 37, "Now when they heard this, they were pricked in their heart."

4. A Doctor's Challenge. Luke 1: 35, "The Holy Ghost shall come upon thee, and the power of the Highest shall overshadow thee."

5. The Master's Challenge. Matt. 19: 21, "If thou wilt be perfect, go and sell that thou hast, and give to the poor."

CHARACTERISTICS OF GOD

1. The Finger of God. Ex. 8: 19, "This is the finger of God."

2. The Face of God. Gen. 32: 30, "And Jacob called the name of the place Peniel: for I have seen God face to face."

3. The Hand of God. II Chron. 30: 12, "Also in Judah the hand of God was to give them one heart to do the commandment of the king."

4. The Arms of God. Deut. 33: 27, "The eternal God is thy refuge, and underneath are the everlasting arms."

5. The Eyes of God. II Chron. 16: 9, "For the eyes of the Lord run to and fro throughout the whole earth."

PROMISES OF CONFIDENCE

1. A Secret Place. Ps. 91: 1, "He that dwelleth in the secret place of the most High shall abide under the shadow of the Almighty."

2. A Present Help. Ps. 46: 1, "God is our refuge and strength, a very present help in trouble."

3. A Keeping Power. Ps. 91: 11, "For he shall give his angels charge over thee, to keep thee in all thy ways."

4. An Enduring Presence. Matt. 28: 20, "And, lo, I am with you alway, even unto the end of the world."

GREATER EVANGELISM

1. A Sinful Man. Ps. 38: 8, "I am feeble and sore broken."

2. A Converted Woman. Acts 16: 14, "And a certain woman named Lydia, a seller of purple."

3. A Distant Disciple. Matt. 26: 58, "But Peter followed him afar off unto the high priest's palace."

4. A Changed Rebel. Acts 26: 15, "And he said, I am Jesus whom thou persecutest."

5. An Inviting Friend. Rev. 22: 17, "And let him that is athirst come. And whosoever will, let him take the water of life freely."

6. A Matchless Father. Luke 12: 30, "Your Father knoweth that ye have need of these things."

7. A Triumphant King. Matt. 2: 2, "Where is he that is born King of the Jews?"

DUTIES OF CHRISTIANS

1. To Sacrifice. II Chron. 5:6, "All the congregation of Israel that were assembled unto him before the ark, sacrificed sheep and oxen."

2. To Pray. Dan. 6: 10, "And gave thanks before his God, as he did aforetime."

3. To Attend Church. Ps. 27: 4, "That I may dwell in the house of the Lord all the days of my life."

4. To Maintain Sound Doctrine. I Tim. 4: 16, "Take heed unto thyself, and unto the doctrine; continue in them."

5. To Observe Communion. Luke 22: 19, "This is my body which is given for you: this do in remembrance of me."

6. To Bear Fruit. John 15: 16, "That ye should go and bring forth fruit, and that your fruit should remain."

TRAFFIC SIGNS OF THE BIBLE

1. Do Not Stop on Pavement. I Cor. 8: 10, "For if any man see thee which hast knowledge sit at meat in the idol's temple, shall not the conscience of him which is weak be emboldened."

2. Detour 500 Feet. Ex. 3: 1, "And he led the flock to the backside of the desert, and came to the mountain of God."

3. No U Turns. Luke 9: 62, "No man, having put his hand to the plow, and looking back, is fit for the kingdom of God."

4. Safety Zone. Prov. 8: 13, "The fear of the Lord is to hate evil . . ."

5. Stop! Look! Listen!. Prov. 8: 34, "Blessed is the man that heareth me, watching daily at my gates, waiting at the posts of my doors."

6. Safety First, Keep to the Right. Deut. 6: 18, "And thou shalt do that which is right and good in the sight of the Lord."

7. Hospital Zone. Luke 10: 33-37, "But a certain Samaritan . . . . "

8. No Parking. Matt. 26: 69, "Now Peter sat without in the palace."

9. This Road is Patrolled. II Chron. 16: 9, "For the eyes of the Lord run to and fro throughout the whole earth."

10. Slow Down, School Children. Mark 10: 14, "Suffer the little children to come unto me, and forbid them not: for of such is the kingdom of God."

11. Miles to Eternity. Ps. 90: 10, "The days of our years are threescore years and ten; and if by reason of strength they be fourscore years, yet is their strength labour and sorrow."

IMPORTANT BIBLE GATES

1. An Iron Gate. Acts 12: 10, "When they were past the first and second ward, they came unto the iron gate that leadeth unto the city."

2. A Straight Gate. Matt. 7: 13, "Enter ye in at the strait gate: for wide is the gate, and broad is the way, that leadeth to destruction."

3. The Gates of Hell. Matt. 16: 18, "And the gates of hell shall not prevail against it."

4. The Beautiful Gate. Acts 3: 6, "Then Peter said, Silver and gold have I none; but such as I have give I thee."

5. The Gate of Heaven. Gen. 28: 17, "This is none other but the house of God, and this is the gate of heaven."

CHRISTIAN LIBERTIES

1. The Liberty of Law. James 1: 25, "But whoso looketh into the perfect law of liberty, . . . this man shall be blessed in his deed."

2. Limitations of Liberty. I Cor. 6: 12, "All things are lawful unto me, but all things are not expedient."

3. The Liberty of Faultfinding. Matt. 7: 5, "Thou hypocrite, first cast out the beam out of thine own eye."

4. The Liberty of the Prodigal. Luke 15: 20, "And he arose, and came to his father."

5. The Liberty of the Elder Brother. Luke 15: 31, "And he said unto him, Son, thou art ever with me, and all that I have is thine."

TESTED CHRISTIANS

1. The Test of Discipleship. I John 3: 14, "He that loveth not his brother abideth in death."

2. The Test of Faith. Heb. 11: 17, "By faith Abraham, when he was tried, offered up Isaac."

3. The Test of Ridicule. I Peter 4: 14, "If ye be reproached for the name of Christ, happy are ye."

4. The Test of Modernism. II Tim. 3: 14, "But continue thou in the things which thou hast learned and hast been assured of."

5. The Test of Motherhood. I Kings 3: 27, "Give her the living child, and in no wise slay it: she is the mother thereof."

6. The Test of Affliction. Ps. 119: 71, "It is good for me that I have been afflicted; that I might learn thy statutes."

SO CALLED "RESPECTABLE SINS"

1. Talebearing. Prov. 11: 13, "A talebearer revealeth secrets: but he that is of a faithful spirit concealeth the matter."

2. Thought Adultery. Matt. 5: 28, "Whosoever looketh on a woman to lust after her hath committed adultery with her already in his heart."

3. Faultfinding. Matt. 6: 3, "But when thou doest alms, let not thy left hand know what thy right hand doeth."

4. Form of Godliness. II Tim. 3: 5, "Having a form of godliness, but denying the power thereof."

5. Unforgiving Spirit. Matt. 6: 15, "But if ye forgive not men their trespasses, neither will your Father forgive your trespasses."

6. Neglecting Salvation. Heb. 2: 3, "How shall we escape, if we neglect so great salvation."

7. Desecrating the Lord's Day. Ex. 20: 8, "Remember the sabbath day, to keep it holy."

THE IDEAL CHURCH

1. The Ideal Elder. I Tim. 4: 16, "Take heed unto thyself, and unto the doctrine."

2. The Ideal Deacon. Acts 6: 3, "Men of honest report, full of the Holy Ghost and wisdom."

3. The Ideal Christian. I Tim. 6: 12, "Fight the good fight of faith, lay hold on eternal life, whereunto thou art also called, and hast professed a good profession before many witnesses."

4. The Ideal Preacher. I Tim. 6: 12, "Fight the good fight of faith, lay hold on eternal life, whereunto thou art also called."

5. The Ideal Congregation. Acts 2: 42, "And they continued stedfastly in the apostles' doctrine and fellowship, and in breaking of bread, and in prayers."

6. The Ideal God. Ps. 89: 6, "For who in heaven can be compared unto the Lord? who among the sons of the mighty can be likened unto the Lord?"

BAD CHURCH MEMBERS

1. Border-Line Christians. Rev. 2: 16, "Repent; or else I will come unto thee quickly."

2. Top-Heavy Christians. I John 4: 1, "Try the spirits whether they are of God: because many false prophets are gone out into the world."

3. Unconverted Followers. Luke 22: 31, "And the Lord said, Simon, Simon, behold, Satan hath desired to have you, that he may sift you as wheat."

4. Home-Breaking Christians. Prov. 11: 29, "He that troubleth his own house shall inherit the wind."

5. Troublesome Christians. I Cor. 14: 40, "Let all things be done decently and in order."

6. Rocking-Chair Christians. Amos 6: 1, "Woe to them that are at ease in Zion."

7. Gossipping Christians. I Tim. 5: 13, "And not only idle, but tattlers also and busybodies, speaking things which they ought not."

8. Floating Christians. II Tim. 4: 3, "For the time will come when they will not endure sound doctrine; . . . shall they heap to themselves teachers, having itching ears."

9. Stumbling-Block Christians. Rom. 14: 13, "That no man put a stumbling block or an occasion to fall in his brother's way."

NOTHING

1. Nothing but Leaves. Mark 11: 13, "And seeing a fig tree afar off having leaves, he came, if haply he might find any thing thereon."

2. Nothing but Stones. Luke 4: 3, "And the devil said unto him, If thou be the Son of God, command this stone that it be made bread."

3. Nothing but a Brass Band. I Cor. 13: 1, "I am become as sounding brass, or a tinkling cymbal."

4. Nothing but Death. I Kings 19: 4, "And he requested for himself that he might die."

5. Nothing but the Undertaker. Acts 5: 6, "And the young men arose, wound him up, and carried him out, and buried him."

6. Nothing but Cheapening the Gospel. II Cor. 3: 9, "For if the ministration of condemnation be glory, much more doth the ministration of righteousness exceed in glory."

7. Nothing but Hell. Matt. 25: 41, "Depart from me, ye cursed, into everlasting fire, prepared for the devil and his angels."

COMMUNICATIONS OF GOD

1. The Voice of God. I Kings 19: 12, "And after the earthquake a fire; but the Lord was not in the fire: and after the fire a still small voice."

2. The Prophets of God. II Peter 1: 19, "We have also a more sure word of prophecy."

3. God's World of Nature. Ps. 19: 1, "The heavens declare the glory of God; and the firmament sheweth his handywork."

4. God's Written Revelation. Deut. 29: 29, "But those things which are revealed belong unto us and to our children for ever."

5. The Son of God. Heb. 1: 2, "Hath in these last days spoken unto us by his Son."

6. The Spirit of God. I Cor. 2: 10, "But God hath revealed them unto us by his Spirit."

GOOD AND BAD FOUNDATIONS

1. A Sure Foundation. Isa. 28: 16, "Behold, I lay in Zion for a foundation a stone, a tried stone, a precious corner stone, a sure foundation."

2. An Insecure Foundation. Ezek. 13: 11, "Say unto them which daub it with untempered morter, that it shall fall."

3. A Foundation with a Seal. II Tim. 2: 19, "Nevertheless the foundation of God standeth sure."

4. A Firm Foundation. Matt. 8: 24, "And, behold, there arose a great tempest in the sea."

5. A Foundation of Sand. Matt. 8: 27, "What manner of man is this, that even the winds and the sea obey him!"

HOW APPROACH DEATH?

1. Appointed to Die. Heb. 9: 28, "So Christ was once offered to bear the sins of many; and unto them that look for him shall he appear the second time without sin unto salvation."

2. A Glass Darkly. I Cor. 13: 12, "For now we see through a glass, darkly; but then face to face."

3. Believe in Me. John 14: 1, "Let not your heart be troubled: ye believe in God, believe also in me."

4. Commit My Spirit. Ps. 31: 5, "Into thine hand I commit my spirit: thou hast redeemed me, O Lord God of truth."

5. My Redeemer Liveth. John 20: 25, "We have seen the Lord."

GOD'S SPIRITUAL GIFTS

1. A New Heart. Ezek. 11: 19, "And I will give them one heart, and I will put a new spirit within you."

2. Faith. Eph. 2: 8, "For by grace are ye saved through faith; and that not of yourselves: it is the gift of God."

3. Rest. II Thess. 1: 7, "And to you who are troubled rest with us, when the Lord Jesus shall be revealed from heaven with his mighty angels."

4. Grace. Ps. 84: 11, "The Lord will give grace and glory."

5. Righteousness. Rom. 5: 17, "Abundance of grace and of the gift of righteousness."

6. Strength. Ps. 68: 35, "The God of Israel is he that giveth strength and power unto his people."

7. A New Prophet. Deut. 18: 15, "The Lord thy God will raise up unto thee a Prophet from the midst of thee."

REQUIREMENTS OF DISCIPLESHIP

1. Give your Heart. Prov. 2: 2, "So that thou incline thine ear unto wisdom, and apply thine heart to understanding."

2. Love the Lord. Matt. 22: 37, "Thou shalt love the Lord thy God with all thy heart, and with all thy soul, and with all thy mind."

3. Follow Christ. John 10: 27, "My sheep hear my voice, and I know them, and they follow me."

4. Pray without Ceasing. I Thess. 5: 17, "Pray without ceasing."

5. Run with Patience. Heb. 12: 1, "And let us run with patience the race that is set before us."

6. Serve Others. Gal. 6: 10, "Let us do good unto all men, especially unto them who are of the household of faith."

THE STRUGGLE OF LIFE

1. Afflictions. II Cor. 12: 7, "There was given to me a thorn in the flesh, the messenger of Satan to buffet me, lest I should be exhalted above measure."

2. Temptations. James 1: 2, "My brethren, count it all joy when ye fall into divers temptations."

3. Ambitions. Luke 22: 24, "And there was also a strife among them, which of them should be accounted the greatest."

4. Weaknesses. Rom. 7: 15, "For that which I do I allow not: for what I would, that I do not; but what I hate, that I do."

5. Death. II Cor. 1: 9, "But we had the sentence of death in ourselves, that we should not trust in ourselves, but in God which raiseth the dead."

6. Destiny. Ps. 90: 10, "The days of our years are threescore years and ten."

QUALITIES OF LOVE

1. Love Covers Sin. Prov. 10: 12, "Hatred stirreth up strifes: but love covereth all sins."

2. Love is as Strong as Death. Song of Sol. 8: 6, "Set me as a seal upon thine heart, as a seal upon thine arm: for love is strong as death."

3. Love Worketh no Ill. Rom. 13: 10, "Love worketh no ill to his neighbour: therefore love is the fulfilling of the law."

4. Love Comes from God. I John 4: 7, "Beloved, let us love one another: for love is of God."

5. Our Love Waxes Cold. Matt. 24: 12, "And because iniquity shall abound, the love of many shall wax cold."

BIBLE TRUTHS ABOUT SATAN

1. Satan Fell as Lightning. Luke 10: 18, "And he said unto them, I beheld Satan as lightning fall from heaven."

2. Satan Provoked David. I Chron. 21: 1, "And Satan stood up against Israel, and provoked David to number Israel."

3. Satan-Filled Hearts. Acts 5: 3, "Why hath Satan filled thine heart to lie to the Holy Ghost?"

4. Buffetings of Satan. II Cor. 12: 7, "A thorn in the flesh, the messenger of Satan to buffet me."

5. Satan's Doom. Col. 2: 15, "And having spoiled principalities and powers, he made a shew of them openly, triumphing over them in it."

LIFE'S ALL IMPORTANT CHOICES

1. God or Baal. I Kings 18: 21, "How long halt ye between two opinions?"

2. Christ or Barabbas. Matt. 27: 17, "Whom will ye that I release unto you? Barabbas, or Jesus which is called Christ?"

3. The World or Your Soul. Matt. 16: 26, "For what is a man profited, if he shall gain the whole world, and lose his own soul?"

4. Life or Death. Jer. 8: 3, "And death shall be chosen rather than life by all the residue of them that remain of this evil family."

5. Heaven or Hell. John 5: 29, "They that have done good, unto the resurrection of life; and they that have done evil, unto the resurrection of damnation."

CONSECRATED CHASTENING

1. Chastening is of God. Deut. 8: 5, "Thou shalt also consider in thine heart, that, as a man chasteneth his son, so the Lord thy God chasteneth thee."

2. Corrective Chastening. Prov. 3: 12, "For whom the Lord loveth he correcteth; even as a father the son in whom he delighteth."

3. Merciful Chastening. Isa. 54: 7, "For a small moment have I forsaken thee; but with great mercies will I gather thee."

4. Prayerful Chastening. Ps. 50: 15, "And call upon me in the day of trouble: I will deliver thee, and thou shalt glorify me."

THE LORD OF BODY ACTION

1. Keep Thy Tongue. Ps. 34: 13, "Keep thy tongue from evil, and thy lips from speaking guile."

2. Hearing Ears. Prov. 10: 17, "He is in the way of life that keepeth instruction: but he that refuseth reproof erreth."

3. Cleansed Hands. James 4: 8, "Cleanse your hands, ye sinners; and purify your hearts."

4. Understanding Heart. I Kings 3: 9, "Give therefore thy servant an understanding heart to judge thy people."

5. Lifted heads. Ps. 110: 7, "He shall drink of the brook in the way: therefore shall he lift up the head."

6. Directed Feet. Prov. 4: 26: "Ponder the path of thy feet, and let all thy ways be established."

BLESSED ASSURANCE

1. Assured of God's Love. John 3: 16, "For God so loved the world, that he gave. . . ."

2. Assured of Sonship. I John 3: 2, "Beloved, now are we the sons of God.

3. Assured of Eternal Life. John 10: 28, "And I give unto them eternal life; and they shall never perish."

4. Assured of Security. Ps. 125: 1, "They that trust in the Lord shall be as mount Zion, which cannot be removed, but abideth for ever."

5. Assured of the Scriptures. II Tim. 3: 15, "And that from a child thou hast known the holy scriptures."

BLESSINGS IN DEATH

1. Victory Over Death. I Cor. 15: 57, "But thanks be to God, which giveth us the victory through our Lord Jesus Christ."

2. Resurrection and Life. John 11: 25, "I am the resurrection, and the life."

3. Death is Gain. Phil. 1: 21, "For to me to live is Christ, and to die is gain."

4. More Than Conquerors. Rom. 8: 37, "Nay, in all these things we are more than conquerors through him that loved us."

5. An Eternal House. II Cor. 5: 1, "We have a building of God, an house not made with hands, eternal in the heavens."

REVEALED REALITIES

1. Revealed Glory. Isa. 40: 5, "And the glory of the Lord shall be revealed, and all flesh shall see it together."

2. Revealed Peace. Jer. 33: 6, "I will cure them, and will reveal unto them the abundance of peace and truth."

3. Revealed Secrets. Dan. 2: 22, "He revealeth the deep and secret things."

4. Revealed Righteousness. Rom. 1: 17, "For therein is the righteousness of God revealed from faith to faith."

5. Revealed Wrath. Rom. 1: 18, "For the wrath of God is revealed from heaven against all ungodliness."

6. Revealed Christ. Gal. 1: 16, "To reveal his Son in me, that I might preach him among the heathen."

Chapter III
CHAPTER CONNECTED SERIES

The title of this chapter refers to a series of sermons based on great chapters of the Bible. There are outstanding chapters of the Bible and one can use these with blessing as a series of sermons. In such a case the exposition of a given chapter should be based on a key text contained in the chapter and the sub-divisions based on paragraphs or blocks of verses found in the chapter. Thus the chapter will be presented as a unit by blending mass detail under main points and sub-points to show the grand sweep of God's word on important themes. Such preaching will require that the minister be fully aware of the relation of the chapter to the entire book of the Bible from which it is taken and that this relationship be portrayed in the exposition of the chapter selected.

There are parts of the Bible that lend themselves particularly well to this kind of exposition. While we realize that the numbering of the Bible chapter and verses was executed without supposed inspiration, yet it is true that wonderful units have manifested themselves in the actual chapter demarkation of the Scriptures into the chapters as we know them today in our Bibles. Not only in the Psalms but in other chapters, sections of the Bible afford excellent bases for series to follow for inspiration and instruction.

There is a second kind of chapter series which is also profitable for spiritual blessing. This kind presents the Word of God in an entire series of sermons on a given chapter of the Bible. There are many excellent chapters which lend themselves to such serial exposition as will be demonstrated in this chapter.

SPIRITUAL POSSESSIONS – I PETER 1

1. Dispersion. Vs. 1, "To the strangers scattered."

2. Our Trinity. Vs. 2, "Elect according to the foreknowledge of God the Father, through sanctification of the Spirit . . . the blood of Jesus."

3. Our Inheritance. Vs. 4, "To an inheritance incorruptible, and undefiled, and that fadeth not away, reserved in heaven for you.

4. Our Faith Trial. Vs. 7, "That the trial of your faith, being much more precious than of gold that perisheth."

5. Our Salvation. Vs. 9, "Receiving the end of your faith, even the salvation of your souls."

6. Our Revealed Prophecy. Vs. 10, "Of which salvation the prophets have enquired and searched diligently."

7. Our Holiness. Vs. 16, "Be ye holy; for I am holy."

8. Our Calling on God. Vs. 17, "Call on the Father, who without respect of persons judgeth according to every man's work."

9. Our Loving the Brethren. Vs. 22, "Seeing ye have purified your souls in obeying the truth through the Spirit unto unfeigned love of the brethren."

DIRECTIVES FOR CHRISTIAN LIVING – EPHESIANS 6: 1-10

1. Children, Obey Your Parents. Vs. 1, "Children, obey your parents in the Lord: for this is right."

2. Fathers, Provoke Not Your Children. Vs. 4, "Fathers, provoke not your children to wrath."

3. Servants, Serve with Goodwill. Vs. 5, "Servants, be obedient to them that are your masters according to the flesh."

4. Masters, Forebear. Vs. 9, "And, ye masters, do the same things unto them, forbearing threatening: knowing that your Master also is in heaven."

5. Christians, Be Strong. Vs. 10, "Be strong in the Lord, and in the power of his might."

SPIRITUAL WEAPONS – EPHESIANS 6: 11-17

1. The Girdle of Truth. Vs. 14, "Stand therefore, having your loins girt about with truth."

2. The Breastplate of Righteousness. Vs. 14, ". . . and having on the breastplate of righteousness."

3. The Shoes of Preparation. Vs. 15, "And your feet shod with the preparation of the gospel of peace."

4. The Shield of Faith. Vs. 16, "Above all, taking the shield of faith."

5. The Helmet of Salvation. Vs. 17, "And take the helmet of salvation."

6. The Sword of the Spirit. Vs. 17, ". . . and the sword of the Spirit, which is the word of God."

PSALMS IN DAILY LIFE

1. A Psalm of Contrast. Ps. 1: 6, "For the Lord knoweth the way of the righteous: but the way of the ungodly shall perish."

2. A Psalm of Care. Ps. 103: 13, "Like as a father pitieth his children, so the Lord pitieth them that fear him."

3. A Psalm of Conflict. Ps. 73: 16, "When I thought to know this, it was too painful for me."

4. A Psalm of Compassion. Ps. 32: 1, "Blessed is he whose transgression is forgiven, whose sin is covered."

5. A Psalm of Consecration. Ps. 112: 3, "And his righteousness endureth forever."

THE SAVIOUR PROPHESIED – ISAIAH 53

1. Despised and Rejected. Vs. 3, "He is despised and rejected of men; a man of sorrows, and acquainted with grief."

2. Smitten of God. Vs. 4, "Yet we did esteem him stricken, smitten of God, and afflicted."

3. Wounded for Us. Vs. 5, "But he was wounded for our transgressions, he was bruised for our iniquities."

4. Cut off for Transgression. Vs. 8, "For he was cut off out of the land of the living."

5. Bruised for Sin. Vs. 10, "Yet it pleased the Lord to bruise him; he hath put him to grief."

6. Travail Satisfied. Vs. 11, "He shall see of the travail of his soul, and shall be satisfied."

7. Intercession Made. Vs. 12, "And he bare the sin of many, and made intercession for the transgressors."

OUR POSSESSIONS WITH GOD – ROMANS 5

1. Peace. Vs. 1, "Therefore being justified by faith, we have peace with God."

2. Salvation. Vs. 9, "Much more then, being now justified by his blood, we shall be saved from wrath through him."

3. Grace. Vs. 15, "But not as the offence, so also is the free gift."

4. Eternal Life. Vs. 21, "Even so might grace reign through righteousness unto eternal life by Jesus Christ our Lord."

NEGATIVE ASSERTIONS – ROMANS 8

1. No Condemnation. Vs. 1, "There is therefore now no condemnation to them which are in Christ Jesus."

2. No Walking after the Flesh. Vs. 6, "For to be carnally minded is death; but to be spiritually minded is life and peace."

3. No Spiritual Bondage. Vs. 15, "For ye have not received the spirit of bondage again to fear."

4. No Knowledge of Self and Life. Vs. 27, "And he that searcheth the hearts knoweth what is the mind of the Spirit."

5. No Separation from Christ. Vs. 35, "Who shall separate us from the love of Christ?"

SPIRITUAL ALTERATIONS – JOHN 3

1. Two Teachers. Vs. 2, "Thou art a teacher come from God." Vs. 10, "Art thou a master of Israel, and knowest not these things?"

2. Two Births. Vs. 6, "That which is born of the flesh is flesh; and that which is born of the Spirit is spirit."

3. Two Birth Agents. Vs. 5, "Except a man be born of water and of the Spirit, he cannot enter into the kingdom of God."

4. Two Realms. Vs. 12, "If I have told you earthly things, and ye believe not, how shall ye believe, if I tell you of heavenly things?"

5. Two Deliverances. Vs. 14, "And as Moses lifted up the serpent in the wilderness, even so must the Son of man be lifted up."

6. Two Peoples. Vs. 15, "That whosoever believeth in him should not perish, but have eternal life."

7. Two Results. Vs. 17, "For God sent not his Son into the world to condemn the world; but that the world through him might be saved."

8. Two Forces. Vs. 20-21, "For every one that doeth evil hateth the light . . . But he that doeth truth cometh to the light."

9. Two Ministers. Vs. 28, "Ye yourselves bear me witness, that I said, I am not the Christ, but that I am sent before him."

10. Two ways. Vs. 36, "He that believeth on the Son hath everlasting life: and he that believeth not the Son shall not see life."

BEGINNINGS

1. Beginning of the World. Gen. 1: 1, "In the beginning God created the heaven and the earth."

2. Beginning of Man. Gen. 1: 26, "And God said, Let us make man in our image, after our likeness."

3. Beginning of the Sabbath. Gen. 2: 3, "And God blessed the seventh day, and sanctified it."

4. Beginning of Woman. Gen. 2: 22, "And the rib, which the Lord God had taken from man, made he a woman, and brought her unto the man."

5. Beginning of Satan's Appearance. Gen. 3: 1, "Now the serpent was more subtle than any beast of the field."

6. Beginning of Sin. Gen. 3: 6, "And did eat, and gave also unto her husband with her; and he did eat."

7. Beginning of Judgment. Gen. 3: 17, "Cursed is the ground for thy sake; in sorrow shalt thou eat of it all the days of thy life."

8. Beginning of Gospel Promise. Gen. 3: 15, "I will put enmity between thee and the woman, and between thy seed and her seed."

AFFIRMATIONS FROM JOB

1. About Man's Condition. Job 1: 21, "Naked came I out of my mother's womb, and naked shall I return thither."

2. About Man's Relation to Satan. Job 2: 3, "And the Lord said unto Satan, Hast thou considered my servant Job?"

3. About Man's Grief. Job 6: 2, "Oh that my grief were throughly weighed, and my calamity laid in the balances together."

4. About Man's Relation to God. Job 9: 2, "I know it is so of a truth: but how should man be just with God?"

5. About Man's Redeemer. Job 19: 25, "For I know that my redeemer liveth, and that he shall stand at the latter day upon the earth."

REVELATION THROUGH ISAIAH

1. About Man's Sin. Isa. 1: 4, "Ah sinful nation, a people laden with iniquity."

2. About Man's Vision. Isa. 6: 8, "Also I heard the voice of the Lord, saying, Whom shall I send, and who will go for us? Then said I, Here am I, send me."

3. About Man's Deliverance. Isa. 9: 6, "For unto us a child is born, unto us a son is given: and the government shall be upon his shoulder."

4. About Man's Praise. Isa. 25: 1, "I will praise thy name; for thou hast done wonderful things."

5. About Man's Comfort. Isa. 40: 1, "Comfort ye, comfort ye my people, saith your God."

6. About Man's Redemption. Isa. 43: 1, "O Israel, Fear not: for I have redeemed thee, I have called thee by thy name; thou art mine."

7. About Man's Suffering Saviour. Isa. 53: 3, "He is despised and rejected of men; a man of sorrows, and acquainted with grief."

8. About Man's Invitation. Isa. 55: 1, "Ho, every one that thirsteth, come ye to the waters."

LOST AND FOUND – LUKE 15

1. Lost Sheep. Vs. 6, "Rejoice with me; for I have found my sheep which was lost."

2. Lost Coin. Vs. 9, "Rejoice with me; for I have found the piece which I had lost."

3. Lost Son. Vs. 32, "For this thy brother was dead, and is alive again; and was lost, and is found."

COMFORT FOR TROUBLED HEARTS – JOHN 14

1. The Promise of Heaven. Vs. 2, "In my Father's house are many mansions."

2. Jesus Points the Way. Vs. 6, "Jesus saith unto him, I am the way, the truth, and the life."

3. The Possibility of Revelation. Vs. 9, "He that hath seen me hath seen the Father."

4. The Power of Prayer. Vs. 14, "If ye shall ask any thing in my name, I will do it."

5. The Promise of the Comforter. Vs. 16, "And I will pray the Father, and he shall give you another Comforter, that he may abide with you for ever."

6. The Prospect of Life. Vs. 19, "But ye see me: because I live, ye shall live also."

7. The Gift of Peace. Vs. 27, "Peace I leave with you, my peace I give unto you."

FELLOWSHIP WITH CHRIST – JOHN 15

1. The True Vine. Vs. 1, "I am the true vine, and my Father is the husbandman."

2. True Branch. Vs. 2, "Every branch in me that beareth not fruit he taketh away."

3. The Secret of Fruitbearing. Vs. 4, "Abide in me, and I in you."

4. The Source of True Joy. Vs. 11, "These things have I spoken unto you, that my joy might remain in you."

5. A Mark of True Love. Vs. 13, "Greater love hath no man than this, that a man lay down his life for his friends."

6. The Proof of True Friendship. Vs. 15, "But I have called you friends; for all things that I have heard of my Father I have made known unto you."

7. Witnesses for Christ. Vs. 27, "And ye also shall bear witness, because ye have been with me from the beginning."

CHRIST'S INTERCESSION – JOHN 17

1. With the Father. Vs. 1, "These words spake Jesus, and lifted up his eyes to heaven."

2. For God's Glory. Vs. 5, "And now, O Father, glorify thou me with thine own self with the glory which I had with thee before the world was."

3. For His Disciples. Vs. 9, "I pray for them . . . for they are thine."

4. For Keeping Power. Vs. 15, "I pray not that thou shouldest take them out of the world, but that thou shouldst keep them from the evil."

5. For All Believers. Vs. 20, "Neither pray I for these alone, but for them also which shall believe on me through their word."

6. For Spiritual Love. Vs. 26, "That the love wherewith thou hast loved me may be in them, and I in them."

POSITIVE PREDICTIONS OF LAST THINGS – MATTHEW 24

1. The Shall of Destruction. Vs. 2, "Verily I say unto you, There shall not be left here one stone upon another."

2. The Shall of Prophesy. Vs. 3, "Tell us, when shall these things be? and what shall be the sign of thy coming, and of the end of the world?"

3. The Shall of False Christs. Vs. 5, "For many shall come in my name, saying, I am Christ; and shall deceive many."

4. The Shall of the World Confusion. Vs. 7, "For nation shall rise against nation, and kingdom against kingdom."

5. The Shall of Persecution. Vs. 9, "Then shall they deliver you up to be afflicted, and shall kill you."

6. The Shall of Endurance. Vs. 13, "He that shall endure unto the end, the same shall be saved."

7. The Shall of Missions. Vs. 14, "And this gospel of the kingdom shall be preached in all the world for a witness unto all nations."

8. The Shall of Great Tribulation. Vs. 21, "For then shall be great tribulation, such as was not since the beginning of the world to this time."

9. The Shall of Christ's Second Coming. Vs. 27, "For as the lightning cometh . . . so shall also the coming of the Son of man be."

10. The Shall of Final Judgment. Vs. 31, "And they shall gather together his elect from the four winds."

11. The Shall of Preparedness. Vs. 44, "Therefore be ye also ready: for in such an hour as ye think not the Son of man cometh."

12. The Shall of Final Separation. Vs. 51, "There shall be weeping and gnashing of teeth."

GOD'S REVELATION – JOHN 1

1. Of His Word. Vs. 1, "In the beginning was the Word, and the Word was with God, and the Word was God."

2. Of His Life. Vs. 4, "In him was life; and the life was the light of men."

3. Of His Light. Vs. 9, "That was the true Light, which lighteth every man."

4. Of His Sonship. Vs. 13, "Which were born, not of blood, nor of the will of the flesh, nor of the will of man, but of God."

5. Of His Glory. Vs. 14, "And we beheld his glory, the glory as of the only begotten of the Father."

6. Of His Grace. Vs. 16, "And of his fulness have all we received, and grace for grace."

7. Of His Revelation. Vs. 18, "No man hath seen God at any time; the only begotten Son, . . he hath declared him."

8. Of His Forerunner. Vs. 23, "He said, I am the voice of one crying in the wilderness."

9. Of His Salvation. Vs. 30, "After me cometh a man which is preferred before me: for he was before me."

10. Of His Record. Vs. 34, "And I saw, and bare record that this is the Son of God."

11. Of His Disciples. Vs. 39, "He saith unto them, Come and see."

12. Of His Insight. Vs. 47, "Behold an Israelite indeed, in whom is no guile!"

13. Of His Angels. Vs. 51, "Hereafter ye shall see heaven open, and the angels of God ascending and descending upon the Son of man."

JOY CHAPTERS FROM PAUL

1. Joy of Salvation. Rom. 10
2. Joy of Worship. I Cor. 11
3. Joy of Suffering. II Cor. 12
4. Joy of Fellowship. Gal. 2
5. Joy of Election. Eph. 1
6. Joy of Satisfied Living. Phil. 4
7. Joy of Consecration. Col. 3
8. Joy of Eternal Comfort. I Thess. 4
9. Joy of Conduct. II Thess. 3
10. Good Citizenship. I Tim. 2
11. Joy of Completed Living. II Tim. 4
12. Joy of Practical Living. Titus 2
13. Joy of Love. Philemon

GREAT CHAPTERS ABOUT SIN AND SALVATION

1. Sin. Gen. 3
2. Law. Ex. 20
3. Suffering Saviour. Isa. 53
4. Praise. Ps. 103
5. Incarnation. Luke 2
6. Comfort. John 14
7. Fellowship. John 15
8. Adoption. Rom. 8
9. Service. Heb. 12
10. Heaven. Rev. 7

PSALMS OF STRUGGLE

1. The Walk of Life. Ps. 1
2. The Walk of Death. Ps. 23
3. The Walk of Adversity. Ps. 73
4. The Walk of Suffering. Ps. 22
5. The Walk of Persecution. Ps. 57
6. The Walk of Deliverance. Ps. 91

PSALMS OF TRUST

1. Trustful Waiting. Ps. 37
2. Trust in God's Help. Ps. 46
3. Trust Amid Fraility. Ps. 39
4. Trust in Blessings. Ps. 103
5. Trust for Deliverance. Ps. 71

PSALMS OF VICTORY

1. Prayer for Victory. Ps. 25
2. Confidence of Victory. Ps. 27
3. Patient Waiting for Victory. Ps. 37
4. Thirst for Victory. Ps. 42
5. Trust for Victory. Ps. 77
6. Thanks for Victory. Ps. 21

PSALMS OF PROVIDENCE

1. The Plan of Nature. Ps. 19
2. The Plan of Preservation. Ps. 16
3. The Plan of Deliverance. Ps. 30
4. The Plan of Security. Ps. 90
5. The Plan of Blessing. Ps. 103
6. The Plan of Devotion. Ps. 116

Chapter IV

BIBLE BOOK SERIES

While the Bible is a single volume it is also a wonderful library. There are several books which lend themselves beautifully to series of sermons. The master exegete can render a great service by presenting a series of sermons on the thought of individual books of the Bible. Some have called this course preaching. It was the practice of the Reformers, who took sections of Scripture and explained them to their people who were famished for the Word of God.

This kind of series means that the minister will have to make a detailed study of the book under consideration. He will need to refresh himself on points of introduction, canonicity, importance in the revelation of God, and relation to other books of the Bible. Having cleared these points he will have to study the book and write out the main emphases to be stressed and the sub-points under these main themes giving basis for his thoughts to unfolding portions of the Scripture in the book chosen. He must avoid the running commentary type of preaching. He must present a unit of the book, a portion of the printed Bible book in relation to the progressive unfolding of the thought of the material under consideration. All of this must be well prepared in advance of announcing the series or beginning to preach the same, or he will run into serious difficulty. When he presents a block of Biblical verses or a portion of the book, he will do well to have a key text for this section so that his people can see and remember relationships of ideas rather than just a mass of explanation concerning the word.

This kind of preaching will suggest many texts to be preached on other occasions. The danger will be that many of these by-product texts will be so attractive that the minister will pause to explain them while he is handling the larger portion or paragraph of the book. He should avoid this temptation. Such golden nugget texts should be noted, filed and kept for later use. Our modern audiences do not desire to be confined, dynamic though it could be, to the book of Numbers for a series of twenty-five weeks. Our modern psychological aversion to this type of serial preaching makes it necessary for the ministers to use tact and forethought in giving instruction on books of the Bible. It can be done in an interesting fashion but it should be more the summary type than the detailed exposition of all parts of the passage. For this time leave the exposition of texts to some later day. It will be a welcome change. It will help both the minister and the people who listen.

The chapter caption indicates <u>Bible</u> book Series. This author is convinced that only <u>Bible</u> book series have a place in the Christian pulpit. He believes that the modern attempt to give book reviews on volumes other than the scripture, and often without Biblical exposition, is an imposition on the Christian gospel and may never be used as a substitute for clear Biblical preaching. Books may be used as reference material to give current and historical light on the sacred word. Excellent illustrative material can be used from books other than the sacred Scriptures, but it must always be secondary to the primary exposition of the Word of life, God's blessing rests on the word which He has spoken and written in our Bible. "For as the rain cometh down, and the snow from heaven, and returneth not thither, but watereth the earth, and maketh it bring forth and bud, that it may give seed to the sower, and bread to the eater: So shall my word be that goeth forth out of my mouth: it shall not return unto me void, but it shall accomplish that which I please, and it shall prosper in the thing whereunto I sent it" (Isa. 55: 10-11). This is God's promise on the Word, the Bible, and not on other books, inspirational as they may be.

Some books, other than Bible books, are based on the Bible and serve as expositions of the Bible. These may be studied chapter by chapter, particularly in Prayer Meeting Series and at other mid-week meetings. More will be stated about this in the chapter which covers this area. When such books are studied it is the intention to explain the Bible itself and glorify God with the same.

THE CALL TO REPENTANCE – JONAH

Jonah's Call to Duty — Chapter 1

1. The Call. Jonah 1: 2, "Arise, go to Nineveh, that great city, and cry against it."

2. The Refusal. Jonah 1: 3, "Jonah rose up to flee unto Tarshish from the presence of the Lord."

3. The Rebuke. Jonah 1: 12, "And he said unto them, Take me up, and cast me forth into the sea."

4. The Preservation. Jonah 1: 17, "Now the Lord had prepared a great fish to swallow up Jonah."

Jonah's Deliverance — Chapter 2

5. His Trouble. Jonah 2: 4, "Then I said, I am cast out of thy sight; yet I will look again toward thy holy temple."

6. His Remembrance. Jonah 2: 7, "When my soul fainted within me I remembered the Lord: and my prayer came in unto thee."

7. His Vow. Jonah 2: 9, "But I will sacrifice unto thee with the voice of thanksgiving."

Jonah Preaches Repentance — Chapter 3

8. Preaching Doom. Jonah 3: 3, "So Jonah arose, and went unto Nineveh, according to the word of the Lord."

9. Repentance Seen. Jonah 3: 5, "So the people of Nineveh believed God, and proclaimed a fast."

10. Relief Experienced. Jonah 3: 10, "And God saw their works . . . and God repented of the evil, that he had said that he would do unto them."

Jonah Learns of God's Love — Chapter 4

11. Take My Life. Jonah 4: 3, "Therefore now, O Lord, take, I beseech thee, my life from me; for it is better for me to die than to live."

12. Glad and Angry. Jonah 4: 6, "So Jonah was exceeding glad of the gourd."

13. Nineveh Spared. Jonah 4: 11, "And should not I spare Nineveh, that great city, wherein are more than six score thousand persons?"

A CALL TO A NEW LIFE – I JOHN

Marks of a New Life – I John 1: 1 thru 2: 25

1. Appropriating Life. I John 1: 2, "For the life was manifested, and we have seen it, and bear witness."

2. Christian Fellowship. I John 1: 3, "That ye also may have fellowship with us."

3. The True Light. I John 1: 5, "And declare unto you, that God is light, and in him is no darkness at all."

4. Walking in the Light. I John 1: 7, "But if we walk in the light, as he is in the light, we have fellowship one with another."

5. Cleansed by Blood. I John 1: 7b, "And the blood of Jesus Christ his Son cleanseth us from all sin."

6. Christ, Our Advocate. I John 2: 1, "And if any man sin, we have an advocate with the Father, Jesus Christ the righteous."

7. Keeping God's Commandments. I John 2: 3, "And hereby we do know that we know him, if we keep his commandments"

8. Brother Love. I John 2: 10, "He that loveth his brother abideth in the light."

9. Spiritual Growth. I John 2: 12, "I write unto you, little children, because your sins are forgiven you for his name's sake."

10. A New Affection. I John 2: 15, "Love not the world, neither the things that are in the world."

11. Faithfulness Amidst Defection. I John 2: 20, "But ye have an unction from the Holy One, and ye know all things."

12. The Promise of Eternal Life. I John 2: 25, "And this is the promise that he hath promised us, even eternal life."

Marks of Sonship – I John 3: 1 thru 5: 5

13. Sons of God. I John 3: 2, "Beloved, now are we the sons of God, and it doth not yet appear what we shall be."

14. Two Classes of Men. I John 3: 10, "In this the children of God are manifest, and the children of the devil. . . ."

15. Brotherly Love. I John 3: 11, "For this is the message that ye heard from the beginning, that we should love one another."

16. Believing in Christ. I John 3: 23, "That we should believe on the name of his son Jesus Christ, and love one another."

17. Testing the Spirits. I John 4: 1, "But try the spirits whether they are of God."

18. Confessing Christ. I John 4: 15, "Whosoever shall confess that Jesus is the Son of God, God dwelleth in him, and he in God."

19. Boldness in the Day of Judgment. I John 4: 17, "Herein is our love made perfect, that we may have boldness in the day of judgment."

20. Victory of Faith. I John 5: 4, "And this is the victory that overcometh the world, even our faith."

Certainties of Sonship – I John 5: 5-18

21. The Witness of God. I John 5: 9, "If we receive the witness of men, the witness of God is greater."

22. Eternal Life. I John 5: 13, "That ye may know that ye have eternal life."

23. Answered Prayer. I John 5: 14, "And this is the confidence that we have in him, that, if we ask any thing according to his will, he heareth us."

24. Sanctification. I John 5: 18, "We know that whosoever is born of God sinneth not."

The Right Attitude toward False Teachers — II John

25. The Salutation. II John 3, "Grace be with you, mercy, and peace, from God the Father, and from the Lord Jesus Christ, the Son of the Father, in truth and love."

26. Walk in His Commandment. II John 6, "And this is love, that we walk after his commandments."

27. Beware of False Teachers. II John 7, "For many deceivers are entered into the world."

28. The Necessity of Self-Inspection. II John 8, "Look to yourselves, that we lose not those things which we have wrought."

29. Abiding in the Doctrine of Christ. II John 9, "He that abideth in the doctrine of Christ, he hath both the Father and the Son."

30. Sharing in Other Men's Sins. II John 11, "For he that biddeth him God speed is partaker of his evil deeds."

The Right Attitude Toward Right Teachers — III John

31. Some First Century Church Members. III John 1, 9, 12.

32. Good Report of a Genuine Christian. III John 3, "For I rejoiced greatly, when the brethren came and testified of the truth that is in thee."

33. Our Duty Toward Faithful Teachers. III John 8, "We therefore ought to receive such, that we might be fellowhelpers to the truth."

34. Not Diotrephes, but Demetrius. III John 11-12, "Demetrius hath good report of all men, and of the truth itself."

LIFE IN THE SPIRIT — GALATIANS

Establishing Apostleship

1. Origin of Apostleship. Gal. 1: 12, "For I neither received it of man, neither was I taught it, but by the revelation of Jesus Christ."

2. Glory of Apostleship. Gal. 1: 24, "And they glorified God in me."

Establishing Affirmations

3. Necessity of Faith. Gal. 3: 24, "Wherefore the law was our schoolmaster to bring us unto Christ, that we might be justified by faith."
4. Possessions of Faith. Gal. 4: 7, "Wherefore thou art no more a servant, but a son."

Establishing Applications

5. Duty for Self. Gal. 5: 16, "Walk in the Spirit, and ye shall not fulfil the lust of the flesh."
6. Duty to Others. Gal. 6: 1, "If a man be overtaken in a fault, ye which are spiritual, restore such an one in the spirit of meekness."

LIFE IN CHRIST – COLOSSIANS

Position of Christ – Chapter 1

1. An Apostle of Jesus Christ. Vs. 1, "Paul, an apostle of Jesus Christ by the will of God."
2. The Father of Jesus Christ. Vs. 3, ". . . the Father of our Lord Jesus Christ."
3. Redemption in Jesus Christ. Vs. 14, "In whom we have redemption through his blood, even the forgiveness of sins."
4. Creation by Jesus Christ. Vs. 16, "For by him were all things created, that are in heaven, and that are in earth."
5. Preeminence of Jesus Christ. Vs. 18, "That in all things he might have the preeminence."
6. Death of Jesus Christ. Vs. 22, "In the body of his flesh through death."
7. Hope of Glory in Jesus Christ. Vs. 27, "Christ in you, the hope of glory."

Sanctification through Christ – Chapter 2

8. Assurance of Understanding in Christ. Vs. 2, "The full assurance of understanding."

9. Stedfastness of Faith in Christ. Vs. 5, "And the stedfastness of your faith in Christ."

10. Walk in Christ. Vs. 6, "As ye have therefore received Christ Jesus the Lord, so walk ye in him."

11. Complete in Christ. Vs. 10, "And ye are complete in him, which is the head of all principality and power."

12. Quickened in Christ. Vs. 13, "And you . . . hath he quickened together with him, having forgiven you all trespasses."

13. Forgiveness of Sins in Christ. Vs. 14, "Blotting out the handwriting of ordinances that was against us."

14. Dead with Christ. Vs. 20, "Wherefore if ye be dead with Christ from the rudiments of the world, why, as though living in the world, are ye subject to ordinances."

Strength with Christ – Chapter 3: 1-17

15. Seek Heavenly Things. Vs. 1, "Seek those things which are above, where Christ sitteth on the right hand of God."

16. Mortify Your Members. Vs. 5, "Mortify therefore your members which are upon the earth."

17. Put Off Evil Practices. Vs. 8, "But now ye also put off all these; anger, wrath, malice, blasphemy, filthy communication out of your mouth."

18. Lie Not One to Another. Vs. 9, "Lie not one to another, seeing that ye have put off the old man with his deeds."

19. Put on the New Man. Vs. 10, "And have put on the new man, which is renewed in knowledge after the image of him that created him."

20. Follow Godly Practices. Vs. 12, "Put on therefore, as the elect of God, holy and beloved, bowels of mercies, kindness, humbleness of mind, meekness, longsuffering."

21. Forbearing One Another. Vs. 13, Forbearing one another, and forgiving one another, if any man have a quarrel against any: even as Christ forgave you, so also do ye."

22. Put on Charity. Vs. 14, "And above all these things put on charity, which is the bond of perfectness."

23. Let Peace Rule. Vs. 15, "And let the peace of God rule in your hearts."

24. Spiritual Songs. Vs. 16, "And admonishing one another in psalms and hymns and spiritual songs, singing with grace in your hearts to the Lord."

25. Do All in Christ's Name. Vs. 17, "And whatsoever ye do in word or deed, do all in the name of the Lord Jesus."

Application – Chapters 3: 18-25

26. Wives, Submit to Husbands. Vs. 18, "Wives, submit yourselves unto your husbands, as it is fit in the Lord."

27. Husbands, Love Wives. Vs. 19, "Husbands, love your wives, and be not bitter against them."

28. Children, Obey. Vs. 20, "Children, obey your parents in all things: for this is well pleasing unto the Lord."

29. Fathers, Provoke Not. Vs. 21, "Fathers, provoke not your children to anger, lest they be discouraged."

30. Servants, Obey. Vs. 22, "Servants, obey in all things your masters according to the flesh."

31. Do All Heartily. Vs. 23, "And whatsoever ye do, do it heartily, as to the Lord, and not unto men."

PASTORAL ADVICE – I TIMOTHY

False Teachers of the Law – I Timothy 1

1. Paul, unto Timothy. I Tim. 1: 2, "Unto Timothy, my own son in the faith."

2. No Other Doctrine. I Tim. 1: 3, "That thou mightest charge some that they teach no other doctrine."

3. The Law Is Good. I Tim. 1: 8, "But we know that the law is good, if a man use it lawfully."

4. The Glorious Gospel. I Tim. 1: 11, "According to the glorious gospel of the blessed God."

5. Mercy Obtained. I Tim. 1: 13, "Who was before a blasphemer, and a persecutor, and injurious; but I obtained mercy."

6. Grace Abundant. I Tim. 1: 14, "And the grace of our Lord was exceeding abundant with faith and love which is in Christ Jesus."

7. A Faithful Saying. I Tim. 1: 15, "This is a faithful saying, and worthy of all acceptation, that Christ Jesus came into the world to save sinners."

8. The King Eternal. I Tim. 1: 17, "Now unto the King eternal, immortal, invisible, the only wise God."

9. Holding Faith and a Good Conscience. I Tim. 1: 19, "Holding faith, and a good conscience."

Proper Worship – I Timothy 2

10. Prayers for All. I Tim. 2: 1, "I exhort therefore, that, first of all, supplications, prayers, intercessions, and giving of thanks, be made for all men."

11. One Mediator. I Tim. 2: 5, "For there is one God, and one mediator between God and men, the man Christ Jesus."

12. Spirit of Prayer. I Tim. 2: 9, "In like manner also, that women adorn themselves in modest apparel, with shamefacedness and sobriety."

13. Women in Worship. I Tim. 2: 11, "Let the woman learn in silence with all subjection."

Duties of Elders and Deacons – I Timothy 3

14. Duties of Elders. I Tim. 3: 7, "Moreover he must have a good report of them which are without; lest he fall into reproach and the snare of the devil."

15. Duties of Deacons. I Tim. 3: 8, "Likewise must the deacons be grave, not doubletongued, not given to much wine, not greedy of filthy lucre."

16. Behavior in God's House. I Tim. 3: 15, "That thou mayest know how thou oughtest to behave thyself in the house of God."

Meeting False Doctrine – I Timothy 4

17. Departing from the Faith. I Tim. 4: 1, "In the latter times some shall depart from the faith."

18. A Good Minister of Jesus Christ. I Tim. 4: 6, "If thou put the brethren in remembrance of these things, thou shalt be a good minister of Jesus Christ."

19. Exercise unto Godliness. I Tim. 4: 7, "But refuse profane and old wives' fables, and exercise thyself rather unto godliness."

20. Labor and Suffer. I Tim. 4: 10, "For therefore we both labour and suffer reproach, because we trust in the living God."

21. An Example of Believers. I Tim. 4: 12, "Be thou an example of the believers, in word, in conversation, in charity, in spirit, in faith, in purity."

22. Meditate on These Things. I Tim. 4: 15, "Meditate upon these things; give thyself wholly to them; that thy profiting may appear to all."

23. Take Heed to Thyself and unto the Doctrine. I Tim. 4: 16, "Take heed unto thyself, and unto the doctrine."

Duties of God's People – I Timothy 5

24. Respect an Elder. I Tim. 5: 1, "Rebuke not an elder, but entreat him as a father."

25. Honor Widows. I Tim. 5: 3, "Honour widows that are widows indeed."

26. Provide for His Own House. I Tim. 5: 8, "But if any provide not for his own, and specially for those of his own house, he hath denied the faith."

27. Avoid Partiality. I Tim. 5: 21, "Observe these things without preferring one before another, doing nothing by partiality."

28. Good Works. I Tim. 5: 25, "Likewise also the good works of some are manifest beforehand."

Personal Problems – I Timothy 6

29. Duty of Servants. I Tim. 6: 1, "Let as many servants as are under the yoke count their own masters worthy of all honor."

30. Doctrine According to Godliness. I Tim. 6: 3, "Even the words of our Lord Jesus Christ, and to the doctrine which is according to godliness."

31. Godliness with Contentment. I Tim. 6: 6, "But godliness with contentment is great gain."

32. The Love of Money. I Tim. 6: 10, "For the love of money is the root of all evil."

33. Fight the Good Fight. I Tim. 6: 12, "Fight the good fight of faith, lay hold on eternal life."

34. The Only Potentate. I Tim. 6: 15, "And only Potentate, the King of kings, and Lord of lords."

35. A Charge to the Rich. I Tim. 6: 17, "Charge them that are rich in this world, that they be not highminded."

36. Keep Thy Trust. I Tim. 6: 20, "O Timothy, keep that which is committed to thy trust."

Chapter V
DOCTRINAL SERIES

Preaching a series of doctrinal sermons is of great importance both for the purpose of inspiration and instruction. Some people in our modern day of so called enlightenment rebel at such series of sermons, but the more discerning listener will appreciate them. The fault is not always with the listener. Sometimes we ministers present doctrinal series in dull, unattractive and non-instructional manners.

We should make sure that doctrinal preaching is not confined to the time when we preach a doctrinal series of sermons. There should be doctrine in every sermon that is preached. In some sermons there is more formal doctrine than in others depending on the character of the text. While this is true, it is profitable for ministers to preach distinctly doctrinal series. Some will claim that these are most appropriate at the regular morning service while others feel they can be made so attractive that people will come for the second service because of interest and instruction to be gained. The secret of such appeal is in the preparation and presentation.

It is possible to present a series on a number of doctrines found in a part of the Bible, in a book of the Bible, or even in a given chapter. It is also possible to preach a series of sermons on a given doctrine presenting various phases of this doctrine thus giving variety and consistent instructional foundation for the good of our people. Variety in this kind of series is also the spice of life.

In presenting a series of doctrinal sermons or a doctrinal sermon at any time we must not forget to put it in terminology the modern mind can enjoy and the ordinary man of the street can receive with profit and with interest. Some ministers are afraid to use the old fashioned terms of the Bible, such as: justification, sanctification, conversion, sin, etc. We must maintain our people's knowledge of these Scriptural terms and doctrines and at the same time use modern terminology to bring the truth home to them.

The doctrinal series is closely related to the Doctrinal Standard Series. In some denominations parts of the doctrinal standards are to be used as subjects for preaching. For instance in the denomination of which I am a member the Heidelberg Catechism must be preached once every four years. In the Christian Reformed Church the truth of this doctrinal standard must be preached at one service every Sunday. In other denominations other standards may prevail and other obligations may pertain to them. Even in denominations where the ministers are not obliged to preach on part or all of their doctrinal standards, yet such preaching will bring wonderful spiritual results if done particularly in serial form.

There is always danger when the point or section of a standard of doctrine is preached in a sermon. This author is of the firm opinion that such doctrine must be preached under the division of sermons founded on the Word of God. To take merely a section of doctrine and preach it without a Biblical text as a foundation for exposition, leads to doctrinal preaching that is separated from the Bible rather than based upon it. All depends on the preacher but he must remember again that God's promise of blessing is on the Word of His revelation, not on the word of men no matter how well stated. Make a series of sermons on your doctrinal standards even if you are not required to do so by church law and it will bring you and your people a real blessing.

SPECIFIED SINS

1. Presumptuous Sins. Ps. 19: 13, "Keep back thy servant also from presumptuous sins."

2. Besetting Sins. Heb. 12: 1, "Let us lay aside every weight, and the sin which doth so easily beset us."

3. Personal Sins. Ps. 51: 4, "Against thee, thee only, have I sinned, and done this evil in thy sight."

4. National Sins. Isa. 1: 4, "Ah sinful nation, a people laden with iniquity."

5. Unpardonable Sins. Matt. 12: 31, "But the blasphemy against the Holy Ghost shall not be forgiven unto men."

6. Sins of Youth. Ps. 25: 7, "Remember not the sins of my youth, nor my transgressions."

7. Secret Sins. Ps. 90: 8, "Thou hast set our iniquities before thee, our secret sins in the light of thy countenance."

8. Greater Sins. John 19: 11, "Therefore he that delivered me unto thee hath the greater sin."

EXPLANATION OF SIN

1. Definition of Sin. Rom. 14: 23, "For whatsoever is not of faith is sin."

2. Origin of Sin. Gen. 3: 7, "And the eyes of them both were opened, and they knew that they were naked."

3. Character of Sin. Eph. 5: 11, "And have no fellowship with the unfruitful works of darkness, but rather reprove them."

4. The Sting of Sin. I Cor. 15: 56, "The sting of death is sin; and the strength of sin is the law."

5. Universality of Sin. Gal. 3: 22, "But the scripture hath concluded all under sin."

6. Christ's Sinlessness. II Cor. 5: 21, "For he hath made him to be sin for us, who knew no sin."

7. Mortifying the Flesh. Col. 3: 5, "Mortify therefore your members which are upon the earth."

8. Confession of Sin. I John 1: 9, "If we confess our sins, he is faithful and just to forgive us our sins."

9. Punishment for Sin. Rom. 2: 8, "But unto them that are contentious, and do not obey the truth, but obey unrighteousness, indignation and wrath."

10. Forgiveness of Sin. Luke 7: 47, "Wherefore I say unto thee, Her sins, which are many are forgiven."

FORGIVING SIN

1. Purpose of Forgiveness. Matt. 18: 35, "So likewise shall my heavenly Father do also unto you, if ye from your hearts forgive not every one his brother their trespasses."

2. Prayer of Forgivensss. Luke 23: 34, "Then said Jesus, Father forgive them; for they know not what they do."

3. Promise of Forgiveness. I John 1: 9, "If we confess our sins, he is faithful and just to forgive us our sins."

4. A Call to Forgiveness. Eph. 4: 32, "Be ye kind one to another," tenderhearted, forgiving one another, even as God for Christ's sake hath forgiven you."

5. The Power to Forgive. Luke 5: 24, "But that ye may know that the Son of man hath power upon earth to forgive sins."

LIFE IN THE WORD

1. Born Again by the Word. I Peter 1: 3, "Hath begotten us again unto a lively hope by the resurrection of Jesus Christ from the dead."

2. Sincere Milk of the Word. I Peter 2: 2, "As newborn babes, desire the sincere milk of the word, that ye may grow thereby."

3. Obey the Word. I Peter 3: 1, "That, if any obey not the word, they also may without the word be won by the conversation of their wives."

4. Keep the Word. I John 2: 5, "But whoso keepeth his word, in him verily is the love of God perfected."

CERTIFIED CERTAINTIES

1. I Know God's Help. Ps. 56: 9, "This I know; for God is for me."

2. I Know That My Redeemer Liveth. Job 19: 25, "For I know that my redeemer liveth."

3. I Know the Love of Christ. Eph. 3: 19, "And to know the love of Christ, which passeth knowledge."

4. I Know God's Providence. Rom. 8: 28, "And we know that all things work together for good to them that love God."

5. I Know of My House Eternal. II Cor. 5: 1, "We have a building of God, an house not made with hands, eternal in the heavens."

THE NECESSITY OF GRACE

1. Grace for Salvation. Eph. 2: 8, "For by grace are ye saved through faith; and that not of yourselves: it is the gift of God."

2. Grace for Instruction. Titus 2: 11, "For the grace of God that bringeth salvation hath appeared to all men."

3. Grace for Growth. II Peter 3: 18, "But grow in grace, and in the knowledge of our Lord and Saviour Jesus Christ."

4. Grace for Justification. Rom. 3: 24, "Being justified freely by his grace through the redemption that is in Christ Jesus."

5. Grace for Witnessing. Col. 4: 6, "Let your speech be alway with grace, seasoned with salt, that ye may know how ye ought to answer every man."

6. Grace for Heart Establishment. Heb. 13: 9, "For it is a good thing that the heart be established with grace."

WHAT IS LIFE?

1. Life Created by God. Gen. 1: 26, "And God said, Let us make man in our image, after our likeness."

2. Life Needs Guidance. Ps. 16: 11, "Thou wilt shew me the path of life."

3. Life Requires Trust. Matt. 6: 25, "Take no thought for your life, what ye shall eat, or what ye shall drink."

4. Life Is Hid with God. Col. 3: 3, "For ye are dead, and your life is hid with Christ in God."

SEEKING SALVATION

1. Believe. Acts 17: 31, "Whereof he hath given assurance unto all men in that he hath raised him from the dead."

2. Confess. I John 1: 9, "If we confess our sins, he is faithful and just to forgive us our sins."

3. Receive. John 1: 12, "But as many as received him, to them gave he power to become the sons of God."

4. Repent. Acts 2: 38, "Repent, and be baptized every one of you in the name of Jesus Christ for the remission of sins."

5. Rejoice. Phil. 4: 4, "Rejoice in the Lord alway: and again I say, Rejoice."

HUMAN REFLECTIONS ON GOD

1. As a Father Pities. Ps. 103: 13, "Like as a father pitieth his children, so the Lord pitieth them that fear him."

2. As a Mother Comforts. Isa. 66: 13, "As one whom his mother comforteth, so will I comfort you."

3. As an Eagle Hovers. Deut. 32: 11, "As an eagle stirreth up her nest, fluttereth over her young, spreadeth abroad her wings, taketh them, beareth them on her wings."

4. As a Hen Gathers. Matt. 23: 37, "How often would I have gathered thy children together, even as a hen gathereth her chickens under her wings."

5. As a Refiner Sits. Mal. 3: 3, "And he shall sit as a refiner and purifier of silver."

THE ORDER OF SALVATION

1. External Call. Isa. 55: 1, "Ho, every one that thirsteth, come ye to the waters."

2. Internal Call. John 3: 7, "Marvel not that I said unto thee, Ye must be born again."

3. Conversion. Acts 9: 6, "And he trembling and astonished said, Lord, what wilt thou have me to do?"

4. Adoption. Rom. 8: 14, "For as many as are led by the Spirit of God, they are the sons of God."

5. Assurance. Isa. 43: 2, "When thou passest through the waters, I will be with thee."

6. Sanctification. John 17: 17, "Sanctify them through thy truth: thy word is truth."

7. Glorification. I Peter 1: 11, "When it testified beforehand the sufferings of Christ, and the glory that should follow."

SALVATION FOR SINNERS

1. Salvation Provided by God. Gen. 3: 15, "It shall bruise thy head, and thou shalt bruise his heel."

2. Salvation Completed by Christ. John 19: 30, "He said, It is finished."

3. Salvation Continued by the Spirit. Matt. 1: 20, "For that which is conceived in her is of the Holy Ghost."

4. Salvation Contested by Satan. Matt. 4: 1, "Then was Jesus led up of the spirit into the wilderness to be tempted of the devil."

5. Salvation Confessed by Believers. Rom. 10: 10, "For with the heart man believeth unto righteousness; and with the mouth confession is made unto salvation."

GOD'S LOVE

1. Searching Love. Ps. 139: 1, "O Lord, thou hast searched me, and known me."

2. Protecting Love. Ps. 16: 5, "The Lord is the portion of mine inheritance and of my cup: thou maintainest my lot."

3. Gift of Love. John 3: 16, "For God so loved . . . that he gave. . . ."

4. Redeeming Love. Gal. 3: 13, "Christ hath redeemed us from the curse of the law."

5. Defending Love. Ps. 46: 1, "God is our refuge and strength, a very present help in trouble."

6. Eternal Love. John 10: 28, "And I give unto them eternal life."

CREATIONS

1. Physical Love. Gen. 1: 26, "And God said, Let us make man in our image, after our likeness."

2. Spiritual Love. John 3: 7, "Marvel not that I said unto thee, Ye must be born again."

3. Devotional Love. Jer. 18: 3, "Then I went down to the potter's house, and, behold, he wrought a work on the wheels."

4. Final Love. I John 3: 1, "Behold, what manner of love the Father hath bestowed upon us."

NEW TESTAMENT LIFTS

1. Life. John 17: 3, "And this is life eternal, that they might know thee the only true God, and Jesus Christ."

2. Love. Rom. 5: 8, "But God commendeth his love toward us, in that, while we were yet sinners, Christ died for us."

3. Light. John 8: 12, "Then spake Jesus again unto them, saying, I am the light of the world."

4. Liberty. Gal. 5: 1, "Stand fast therefore in the liberty wherewith Christ hath made us free."

5. Long. Heb. 11: 10, "He looked for a city which hath foundations, whose builder and maker is God."

6. Look. Heb. 12: 2, "Looking unto Jesus the author and finisher of our faith."

FAITH

1. Historical Faith. James 2: 19, "Thou believest that there is one God; thou doest well: the devils also believe, and tremble."

2. Miraculous Faith. Matt. 7: 22, ". . . in thy name have cast out devils? and in thy name done many wonderful works?"

3. Temporary Faith. Matt. 13: 7, "And some fell among thorns; and the thorns sprung up, and choked them."

4. Saving Faith. Acts 16: 31, "And they said, Believe on the Lord Jesus Christ, and thou shalt be saved."

DOCTRINE OF DEATH

1. Death Came by Sin. Rom. 5: 19, "For as by one man's disobedience many were made sinners, so by the obedience of one shall many be made righteous."

2. Death is Universal: For All. Heb. 9: 27, "And as it is appointed unto man once to die, but after this the judgment."

3. Death is Punishment for Sin. Matt. 15: 4, "He that curseth father or mother, let him die the death."

4. Death is Vanquished by Christ. I Cor. 15: 26, "The last enemy that shall be destroyed is death."

5. Death is Unknown in Heaven. Rev. 21: 4, "And there shall be no more death, neither sorrow, nor crying."

OUR ELECTION

1. God Chooses Us. Rom. 9: 17, "For the scripture saith unto Pharaoh, Even for this same purpose have I raised thee up, that I might shew my power in thee."

2. God Predestined the Saviour. Eph. 3: 11, "According to the eternal purpose which he purposed in Christ Jesus our Lord."

3. God Works in Our Hearts. Phil. 2: 13, "For it is God which worketh in you both to will and to do of his good pleasure."

4. God Wants Us to Respond. Phil. 2: 12, "Work out your own salvation with fear and trembling."

CHRISTIAN LOVE

1. Fruit of the Spirit. Rom. 6: 22, "Ye have your fruit unto holiness, and the end everlasting life."

2. Forbears One Another. Eph. 4: 2, "With all lowliness and meekness, with longsuffering, forbearing one another in love."

3. Increases in Christians. I Thess. 3: 12, "And the Lord make you to increase and abound in love one toward another."

4. Stimulates Truth. Eph. 4: 15, "But speaking the truth in love."

5. Conduct is Safe. Eph. 5: 2, "And walk in love, as Christ also hath loved us."

6. Edifies Believers. I Cor. 8: 1, "Knowledge puffeth up, but charity edifieth."

7. Endeavors a New Life. Gal. 2: 20, "Christ liveth in me."

8. Fulfills the Law. Rom. 13: 10, "Therefore love is the fulfilling of the law."

SPIRITUAL GIFTS

1. Diversity of Gifts. I Cor. 6: 17, "But he that is joined unto the Lord is one spirit."

2. Profitless Gifts. I Cor. 13: 1, 2, "Though I speak with the tongues of men and of angels, and have not charity... I am nothing."

3. Co-operation of Gifts. Rom. 12: 4, "For as we have many members in one body, and all members have not the same office."

4. Communication of Gifts. Acts 19: 6, "And they spake with tongues, and prophesied."

BIBLE DOCTRINE

1. Good Doctrine. Prov. 4: 2, "For I give you good doctrine, forsake ye not my law."

2. Winds of Doctrine. Eph. 4: 14, "Be no more children, tossed to and fro, and carried about with every wind of doctrine."

3. Attending to Doctrine. I Tim. 4: 13, "Till I come, give attendance to reading, to exhortation, to doctrine."

4. Adorning the Doctrine. Titus 2: 10, "That they may adorn the doctrine of God our Saviour in all things."

5. An Astonishing Doctrine. Matt. 11: 18, "For John came neither eating nor drinking, and they say, He hath a devil."

6. God's Doctrine. John 7: 16, "Jesus answered them, and said, My doctrine is not mine, but his that sent me."

7. The Apostles' Doctrine. Acts 2: 42, "And they continued stedfastly in the apostles doctrine.

8. Divers Doctrines. Heb. 13: 9, "Be not carried about with divers and strange doctrines. For it is a good thing that the heart be established with grace."

GREAT CHRISTIAN DOCTRINES

1. About God. Gen. 17: 1, "I am the Almighty God; walk before me, and be thou perfect."

2. About Christ. John 1: 18, "The only begotten Son, which is in the bosom of the Father, he hath declared him."

3. About Sin. Rom. 6: 23, "For the wages of sin is death."

4. About Salvation. Acts 4: 12, "Neither is there salvation in any other."

5. About Punishment. Rev. 20: 15, "And whosoever was not found written in the book of life was cast into the lake of fire."

6. About Reward. II Cor. 5: 10, "For we must all appear before the judgment seat of Christ."

7. About Immortality. John 8: 51, "If a man keep my saying, he shall never see death."

INVISIBLE REALITIES

1. The Invisible God. I Tim. 1: 17, "Now unto the King eternal, immortal, invisible, the only wise God, be honour and glory."

2. Invisible Grace. II Cor. 12: 9, "My grace is sufficient for thee."

3. The Invisible Christ. Matt. 28: 20, "And, lo, I am with you alway, even unto the end of the world."

4. The Invisible Revelation. I Cor. 2: 10, "But God hath revealed them unto us by his Spirit."

5. Invisible Things. II Cor. 4: 18, "But at the things which are not seen... are eternal."

6. Invisible Angels. Ps. 91: 11, "For he shall give his angels charge over thee, to keep thee in all thy ways."

7. Invisible Glory. II Cor. 5: 1, "We have a building of God, an house not made with hands, eternal in the heavens."

STRANGE STATEMENTS OF THE OLD THEOLOGY

1. The Skin of Your Teeth. Job 19: 20, "My bone cleaveth to my skin and to my flesh, and I am escaped with the skin of my teeth."

2. A Watery Eye. Lam. 1: 16, "For these things I weep; mine eye runneth down with water."

3. An Old Tree Stump. Dan. 4: 26, "Whereas they commanded to leave the stump of the tree roots."

4. A Bottle in the Smoke. Ps. 119: 83, "For I am become like a bottle in the smoke."

5. Grasshopper Strength. Num. 13: 33, "And we were in our own sight as grasshoppers."

6. Dogs that Cannot Bark. Isa. 56: 10, "They are all dumb dogs, they cannot bark."

7. A Broken Tooth. Prov. 25: 19, "Confidence in an unfaithful man in time of trouble is like a broken tooth."

8. A God Who Winks. Acts 17: 30, "And the times of this ignorance God winked at."

9. Smoother Than Butter. Ps. 55: 21, "The words of his mouth were smoother than butter."

WALKS WITH GOD

1. The Life Walk. Ps. 84: 6, "Who passing through the valley of Baca make it a well."

2. The Death Walk. Ps. 23: 4, "Yea, though I walk through the valley of the shadow of death, I will fear no evil."

3. The Resurrection Walk. Luke 24: 32, "Did not our heart burn within us, while he talked with us by the way?"

4. The Heavenly Walk. Rev. 3: 4, "And they shall walk with me in white: for they are worthy."

BELIEFS WHICH MATTER

1. Belief in the Trinity. I Peter 1: 2, "Elect according to the foreknowledge of God the Father, through sanctification of the Spirit . . . the blood of Jesus Christ."

2. Belief in the Church. I Cor. 12: 13, "For by one Spirit are we all baptized into one body."

3. Belief in the Forgiveness of Sin. Ps. 103: 3, "Who forgiveth all thine iniquities."

4. Belief in the Communion of Saints. I John 1: 7, "We have fellowship one with another."

5. Belief in the Father Almighty. Neh. 9: 6, "Thou, even thou, art Lord alone; thou hast made heaven."

6. Belief in Jesus Christ our Lord. I Tim. 1: 2, "Grace, mercy, and peace, from God our Father and Jesus Christ our Lord."

ATTITUDES TOWARD SALVATION

1. Too Many Hypocrites. Matt. 13: 30, "Let both grow together until the harvest."

2. Why Do We Call Him Christ? John 1: 41, "We have found the Messias, which is, being interpreted, the Christ."

3. I Do Not Need Christ. Rev. 3: 17, "Thou art wretched, and miserable, and poor, and blind, and naked."

4. I Want Christ On My Own Condition. I Kings 5: 12, "And the Lord gave Solomon wisdom, as he promised him."

5. I Am Not Good Enough. Matt. 9: 13, "For I am not come to call the righteous, but sinners to repentance."

6. I Want a Big Change. Acts 9: 6, "And he trembling and astonished said, Lord, what wilt thou have me to do?"

7. I Do Not Have to Belong to Church. John 6: 53, "Except ye eat the flesh of the Son of man, and drink his blood, ye have no life in you."

8. I Want to Wait. I Kings 18: 21, "How long halt ye between two opinions?"

9. I Can't Give up My Worldly Ways. I John 2: 15, "Love not the world, neither the things that are in the world."

FORGOTTEN TRUTHS

1. Predestination. Rom. 9: 18, "Therefore hath he mercy on whom he will have mercy; and whom he will he hardeneth."

2. Once Saved Always Saved. John 10: 28, "And they shall never perish, neither shall any man pluck them out of my hand."

3. The Trinity. Matt. 3: 16-17, "And Jesus, when he was baptized . . . saw the Spirit of God descending like a dove . . . and lo a voice from heaven."

4. Regeneration. John 3: 7, "Marvel not that I said unto thee, Ye must be born again."

5. Water and Spirit Baptism. Luke 3: 16, "I indeed baptize you with water . . . he shall baptize you with the Holy Ghost and with fire."

6. Doubts of Christians. John 20: 25, "Except I shall see in his hands the print of the nails, and put my finger into the print of the nails, and thrust my hand into his side, I will not believe.

7. Seventy Times Seven. Matt. 18: 22, "I say not unto thee, Until seven times: but, Until seventy times seven."

8. Sin Against the Holy Ghost. Matt. 12: 32, "But whosoever speaketh against the Holy Ghost, it shall not be forgiven him."

9. The Second Coming. Matt. 24: 42, "Watch therefore: for ye know not what hour your Lord doth come."

GREAT "WITHOUTS" OF THE BIBLE

1. Without God. Eph. 2: 12, "That at that time ye were without Christ, being aliens from the commonwealth of Israel."

2. Without Blood. Heb. 9: 22, "And without shedding of blood is no remission."

3. Without Faith. Heb. 11: 6, "Without faith it is impossible to please him."

4. Without Money. Isa. 55: 1, "...and he that hath no money; come ye, buy, and eat."

5. Without Holiness. Heb. 12: 14, "Follow peace with all men, and holiness, without which no man shall see the Lord."

UNIVERSAL REALITIES

1. The Sovereignty of God. Rev. 19: 6, "For the Lord God omnipotent reigneth."

2. The Sinfulness of Man. Gen. 3: 13, "And the Lord God said unto the woman, What is this that thou hast done?"

3. The Suffering of Christians. II Cor. 12: 7, "There was given to me a thorn in the flesh, the messenger of Satan to buffet me."

4. Faith Overcomes. I John 5: 4, "And this is the victory that overcometh the world, even our faith."

5. Death for All. Ps. 116: 15, "Precious in the sight of the Lord is the death of his saints."

6. Jesus, the Only Saviour. Acts 4: 12, "For there is none other name under heaven given among men, whereby we must be saved."

Chapter VI

THE LIFE OF CHRIST SERIES

A. The Material for Series

There is an abundance of material on the life of Christ for series of sermons. While His sojourn on earth was not long, His was a special ministry, and His life was full of activity, explanation and service. These were anticipated in the Old Testament prophecies as described in the gospel record, and as demonstrated in the Acts and Epistles as the life of Christ developed. The record contains many of His utterances, the content of His teaching, the important questions He asked and the outstanding events of His person.

B. The Place for Series

There is place for series sermons about Jesus Christ in every part of the seasonal life of the Christian. Series about Him and His teaching touch on every phase of life and cover every circumstance of experience. Many of them carry a corrective doctrinal import and applications to life abound. Series of the life of Christ are necessarily distinctly Christ-centered and therefore should have repeated emphasis. Our Lord Jesus Christ is not only the Captain of our salvation, the Redeemer for sin, and the King of all of life; His life is the pre-eminence in all things and in all of life. For this reason serial preaching in the life of Christ, is not only appropriate but very necessary for sound preaching and balanced spiritual living.

CHRIST'S SABBATH TEACHING

1. Christ Endorsed Necessary Work on the Sabbath. Mark 2: 23, "He went through the corn fields on the sabbath day; and his disciples began, as they went, to pluck the ears of corn."

2. Christ Endorsed Necessary Healing on the Sabbath. Mark 1: 23, "In their synagogue came a man with an unclean spirit; and he cried out."

3. Christ Endorsed Necessary Deeds of Mercy on the Sabbath. Luke 13: 15, "Thou hypocrite, doth not each one of you on the sabbath loose his ox or his ass from the stall, and lead him away to watering?"

4. Christ Endorsed Spiritual Observance of the Sabbath. John 7: 14, "Now about the midst of the feast Jesus went up into the temple, and taught."

CHRIST'S SERMON SUGGESTIONS

1. Settling with an Enemy. Matt. 5: 24, "Leave there thy gift before the altar, and go on thy way; first be reconciled to thy brother, and then come and offer thy gift."

2. Settling Divorce. Matt. 5: 28, "Whosoever looketh on a woman to lust after her hath committed adultery with her already in his heart."

3. Settling an Oath. Matt. 5: 34, "But I say unto you, Swear not at all; neither by heaven; for it is God's throne."

4. Settling Law of Love. Matt. 5: 39, "Whosoever shall smite thee on thy right cheek, turn to him the other also."

5. Settling Stewardship. Matt. 6: 14, "For if ye forgive men their trespasses, your heavenly Father will also forgive you."

6. Settling Prayers of Life. Matt. 6: 5, "When thou prayest, thou shalt not be as the hypocrites are: for they love to pray standing in the synagogues and in the corners of the streets."

7. Settling Worldliness. Matt. 6: 19, "Lay not up for yourselves treasures upon earth, where moth and rust doth corrupt, and where thieves break through and steal."

8. Settling Faultfinding. Matt. 7: 1, "Judge not, that ye be not judged."

DOCTRINE OF CHRIST

1. Promised Messiah. Matt. 3: 14, "I have need to be baptized of thee, and comest thou to me?"

2. Promised Judgment. Matt. 3: 3, "The voice of one crying in the wilderness, Prepare ye the way of the Lord, make his paths straight."

3. Promised Baptism. Luke 3: 16, "He shall baptize you with the Holy Ghost and with fire."

4. Promised Passover. John 1: 29, "Behold the Lamb of God, which taketh away the sin of the world."

5. Promised Son of God. John 1: 34, "And I saw, and bare record that this is the Son of God."

6. The Promised Deliverer. Rom. 11: 26, "And so all Israel shall be saved: as it is written."

THE TEMPTATIONS OF JESUS

1. The Temptation of Physical Comfort or Appetite. Matt. 4: 2 "When he had fasted forty days and forty nights, he was afterward an hungered."

2. The Temptation of Spiritual Presumption or Pride. Matt. 4: 6, "If thou be the Son of God, cast thyself down."

3. The Temptation of Authority. Matt. 4: 9, "He saith unto him, All these things will I give thee, if thou wilt fall down and worship me."

RESULTS OF CHRIST'S TEMPTATIONS

1. It Is Written. Luke 4: 4, "It is written, That man shall not live by bread alone, but by every word of God."

2. Angels Ministered to Him. Mark 1: 13, "And the angels ministered unto him."

3. The Devil Leaves Him for a Season. Luke 4: 13, "And when the devil had ended all the temptation, he departed from him for a season."

4. He Returned in the Power of the Spirit. Luke 4: 14, "And Jesus returned in the power of the Spirit into Galilee."

JESUS CALLED DISCIPLES

1. John's Followers. John 1: 35, "Again the next day after John stood, and two of his disciples."

2. Nicodemus. John 3: 9, "Nicodemus answered and said unto him, How can these things be?"

3. A Samaritan Woman. John 4: 39, "Many of the Samaritans of that city believed on him for the saying of the woman."

4. Fishermen. Mark: 1: 17, "And Jesus said unto them, Come ye after me, and I will make you to become fishers of men."

CHIRST'S HEALING MINISTRY

1. Healing at a Distance by Request. John 4: 50, "Jesus saith unto him, Go thy way; thy son liveth."

2. Healing of a Demon Possessed. Mark 1: 27, "For with authority commandeth he even the unclean spirits, and they do obey him."

3. Healing of Those Who Contacted Him Personally. Luke 4: 38, "Simon's wife's mother was taken with a great fever; and they besought him for her."

4. Healing of People from Crowds. Mark 3: 10, "He had healed many; insomuch that they pressed upon him for to touch him, as many as had plagues."

CHRIST'S VIEW-POINTS

1. At Beginning— Father's Business. Luke 2: 49, "Wist ye not that I must be about my Father's business?"

2. At Mid-Point— Father's Sacrifice. Luke 9: 51, "He stedfastly set his face to go to Jerusalem."

3. At End— Father's Glory. John 17: 22, "And the glory which thou gavest me I have given them; that they may be one, even as we are one."

CHRIST AND GOVERNMENT

1. Supporting Government. Matt. 22: 21, "Render therefore unto Caesar the things which are Caesar's; and unto God the things that are God's."

2. Paying Taxes. Matt. 22: 17, "Tell us therefore, What thinkest thou? Is is lawful to give tribute unto Caesar, or not?"

3. Claiming His Right. Matt. 26: 53, "Thinkest thou that I cannot now pray to my Father, and he shall presently give me more than twelve legions of angels?"

4. Described Evil. John 2: 15, "He drove them all out of the temple, and the sheep, and the oxen; and poured out the changers' money, and overthrew the tables."

5. Greater Than All Rulers. I Tim. 6: 15, "The King of kings and Lord of lords."

EXCUSES OF NO NEED OF CHRIST

1. Not Necessary. Rom. 3: 3, "For what if some did not believe? shall their unbelief make the faith of God without effect?"

2. Not Concerned. Eph. 5: 4, "Neither filthiness, nor foolish talking, nor jesting, which are not convenient: but rather giving of thanks."

3. Not Good Enough. Isa. 1: 18, "Though your sins be as scarlet, they shall be as white as snow."

4. Good Enough. Isa. 53: 6, "All we like sheep have gone astray; we have turned every one to his own way."

5. A Cold Heart. Ezek. 36: 26, "And I will take away the stony heart out of your flesh, and I will give you an heart of flesh."

6. Way Unfamiliar. John 14: 6, "Jesus saith unto him, I am the way, the truth, and the life."

7. A Church Member Already. Luke 7: 23, "Blessed is he, whosoever shall not be offended in me."

8. The Way Closeth. Isa. 42: 16, "And I will bring the blind by a way that they knew not."

EXCUSES OF POSTPONEMENT

1. Not Now. Isa. 55: 6, "Seek ye the Lord while he may be found, call ye upon him while he is near."

2. Too Young. II Tim. 3: 15, "And that from a child thou hast known the holy scriptures, which are able to make thee wise unto salvation."

3. Too Early. Matt. 24: 44, "Therefore be ye also ready: for in such an hour as ye think not the Son of man cometh."

EXCUSES OF PERSONAL OBJECTIONS

1. Open Confession Not Necessary. Matt. 10: 32, "Whosoever therefore shall confess me before men, him will I confess also before my Father which is in heaven."

2. God Will Not Condemn Us. Luke 13: 3b, "Except ye repent, ye shall all likewise perish."

3. Saved by a Good Life. James 2: 10, "For whosoever shall keep the whole law, and yet offend in one point, he is guilty of all."

4. Bible Cannot Be Understood. James 1: 5, "If any of you lack wisdom, let him ask of God, that giveth to all men liberally."

5. All Will Be Saved Anyhow. Matt. 7: 14, "Because strait is the gate, and narrow is the way, which leadeth unto life, and few there be that find it."

EXCUSES INVOLVING CONSECRATION

1. Surrender Old Companions. James 4: 4, "Ye adulterers and adulteresses, know ye not that the friendship of the world is enmity with God?"

2. Surrender Possessions. Mark 8: 36, "For what shall it profit a man, if he shall gain the whole world, and lose his own soul?"

3. Too Hard. I John 5: 3, "For this is the love of God, that we keep his commandments: and his commandments are not grievous."

4. Surrender Worldly Ways. James 4: 4, "Whosoever therefore will be a friend of the world is the enemy of God."

5. Surrender All. Matt. 16: 25, "For whosoever will save his life shall lose it: and whosoever will lose his life for my sake shall find it."

6. I Cannot Hold Out. I Peter 1: 5, "Who are kept by the power of God through faith unto salvation ready to be revealed in the last time."

7. I haven't Finished Sowing Wild Oats. Gal. 6: 7, "God is not mocked: for whatsoever a man soweth, that shall he also reap."

THE CONVERSATIONS OF JESUS

1. To the Blind Man. Mark 10: 52, "And Jesus said unto him, Go thy way; thy faith hath made thee whole."

2. To the Evil Spirit. Mark 5: 18, "He that had been possessed with the devil prayed him that he might be with him."

3. To the Disciples. Luke 9: 28, "He took Peter and John and James, and went up into a mountain to pray."

4. To the Multitude. John 6: 27, "Labour not for the meat which perisheth, but for the meat which endureth unto everlasting life, which the Son of man shall give unto you."

5. To Peter. Matt. 14: 27, "Straightway Jesus spake unto them, saying, Be of good cheer; it is I; be not afraid."

6. To the Pharisees. Matt. 23: 23, "Woe unto you, scribes and Pharisees, hypocrites!"

7. To the Father. John 12: 27, "Now is my soul troubled; and what shall I say? Father, save me from this hour: but for this cause came I unto this hour."

PROPHECIES ABOUT CHRIST'S COMING

1. Born of a Virgin. Isa. 7: 14, "Therefore the Lord himself shall give you a sign; Behold, a virgin shall conceive, and bear a son."

2. Named before Birth. Isa. 7: 14, ". . . And shall call his name Immanuel."

3. Born of Abrahamian Lineage. Gen. 12: 3, "And in thee shall all families of the earth be blessed."

4. Born in Bethlehem. Mic. 5: 2, "But thou, Bethlehem Ephratah . . . out of thee shall he come forth unto me that is to be ruler in Israel."

PROPHECIES ABOUT CHRIST'S PERSON

1. A King. Ps. 72: 10, "The kings of Tarshish and of the isles shall bring presents."

2. A Prophet. Deut. 18: 15, "And the Lord thy God will raise up unto thee a Prophet from the midst of thee."

3. A Judge. II Sam. 23: 3, "He that ruleth over men must be just, ruling in the fear of God."

4. A Spirit Filled Person. Isa. 11: 2, "And the spirit of the Lord shall rest upon him."

5. A Suffering Saviour. Isa. 53: 3, "He is despised and rejected of men; a man of sorrows, and acquainted with grief."

JESUS' QUESTIONS ABOUT PROVIDENCE

1. Life More Than Meat. Matt. 6: 25, 26, "Take no thought for your life, what ye shall eat, nor what ye shall drink; nor yet for your body, what ye shall put on."

2. Adding to Stature. Luke 12: 25, "And which of you with taking thought can add to his stature one cubit?"

3. Thought for Raiment. Matt. 6: 28, "And why take ye thought for raiment? Consider the lilies of the field, how they grow."

4. Good Gifts for Children. Matt. 7: 11, "If ye then, being evil, know how to give good gifts unto your children, how much more shall your Father which is in heaven give good things to them that ask him."

JESUS' QUESTIONS OF DEVOTION

1. Watch One Hour. Matt. 26: 40, "What, could ye not watch with me one hour?"

2. Why Weep? Mark 5: 39, "Why make ye this ado, and weep? the damsel is not dead, but sleepeth."

3. Fasting Bridechamber Children. Mark 2: 19, "Can the children of the bridechamber fast, while the bridegroom is with them?"

JESUS' QUESTIONS ABOUT HIMSELF

1. Why Call Me Good? Matt. 19: 17, "Why callest thou me good? there is none good but one, that is, God."

2. What Think Ye of Christ? Matt. 22: 42, "What think ye of Christ? whose son is he?"

3. Why Call Me Lord? Luke 6: 46, "Why call ye me, Lord, Lord, and do not the things which I say?"

JESUS' QUESTIONS CONCERNING HUMAN DESIRE

1. What Will Ye That I shall do Unto you? Matt. 20: 32, "Jesus stood still, and called them, and said, What will ye that I should do unto you?"

2. What Disputed Ye? Mark 9: 33, "What was it that ye disputed among yourselves by the way?"

3. Who Touched My Clothes? Mark 5: 30, "And said, Who touched my clothes?"

4. Wherefore Art Thou Come? Matt. 26: 50, "Friend, wherefore art thou come? Then came they, and laid hands on Jesus, and took him."

JESUS' QUESTIONS OF FRUITFULNESS

1. Grapes of Thorns? Matt. 7: 16, "Ye shall know them by their fruits."

2. Gift or Altar? Matt. 23: 19, "Ye fools and blind: for whether is greater, the gift, or the altar that sanctifieth the gift?"

3. Faithless Generation. Mark 9: 19, "O faithless generation, how long shall I be with you? how long shall I suffer you? bring him unto me."

4. My Father's Business. Luke 2: 49, "How is it that ye sought me? wist ye not that I must be about my Father's business?"

JESUS' QUESTIONS OF INVESTIGATION

1. What Went Ye Out to See? Matt. 11: 7, "What went ye out into the wilderness to see? A reed shaken with the wind?"

2. Whereunto Liken This Generation? Matt. 11: 16, "But whereunto shall I liken this generation?"

3. How Many Loaves Have Ye? Matt. 15: 34, "Jesus saith unto them, How many loaves have ye?"

4. Why Tempt Ye Me, Ye Hypocrites? Matt. 22: 18, "But Jesus perceived their wickedness, and said, Why tempt ye me, ye hypocrites?"

5. Whose Is This Image? Mark 12: 16, "And he saith unto them, Whose is this image and superscription?"

JESUS' QUESTIONS RELATING TO OTHERS

1. Who Are My Brethren? Matt. 12: 48, "Who is my mother? and who are my brethren?"

2. Whom Say Ye That I Am? Matt. 16: 15, "He saith unto them, But whom say ye that I am?"

3. Compassion on Fellow Servant? Matt. 18: 33, "Shouldest not thou also have had compassion on thy fellowservant, even as I had pity on thee?"

4. Why Trouble Ye the Woman? Matt. 26: 10; "Why trouble ye the woman? for she hath wrought a good work upon me."

5. Which Loves Most? Luke 7: 42, "Tell me therefore, which of them will love him most?"

JESUS' QUESTIONS CONCERNING FAITH

1. Little Faith. Matt. 6: 30, "Shall he not much more clothe you, O ye of little faith?"

2. Able Faith. Matt. 9: 28, "And Jesus saith unto them, Believe ye that I am able to do this?"

3. Understanding Faith. Matt. 13: 51, "Jesus saith unto them, Have ye understood all these things?"

4. Doubting Faith. Matt. 14: 31, "O thou of little faith, wherefore didst thou doubt?"

5. Faithless Generation. Matt. 17: 17, "Then Jesus answered and said, O faithless and perverse generation, how long shall I be with you?"

JESUS' QUESTIONS OF CONDUCT

1. What Do Ye More Than Others? Luke 6: 32, "For if ye love them which love you, what thank have ye? for sinners also love those that love them."

2. Why Behold the Brother's Mote? Luke 6: 41, "Why beholdest thou the mote that is in thy brother's eye, but perceivest not the beam that is in thine own eye?"

3. Wherefore Think Ye Evil? Luke 5: 23, "Whether is easier to say, Thy sins be forgiven thee; or to say, Rise up and walk?"

4. How Can Ye Speak Good Things? Matt. 12: 34, "How can ye, being evil, speak good things?"

5. Didst Thou Not Agree For a Penny? Matt. 20: 13, "Friend, I do thee no wrong: didst not thou agree with me for a penny?"

6. Is Thine Eye Evil? Matt. 20: 15, "Is it not lawful for me to do what I will with mine own? Is thine eye evil, because I am good?"

JESUS' QUESTIONS OF ABILITY

1. Are Ye Able to Drink of the Cup? Matt. 20: 22, "Are ye able to drink of the cup that I shall drink of?"

2. Who Is Faithful? Luke 12: 42, "Who then is that faithful and wise steward, whom his lord shall make ruler over his household?"

3. Where Is Your Faith? Luke 8: 25, "He said unto them, Where is your faith?"

4. Doing God's Will. Matt. 21: 31, "Whether of them twain did the will of his father?"

Chapter VII
LENTEN SERIES

A. The Emphasis of Lent

Lent comes in the Spring of the year and is observed for six weeks or Sundays preceeding Easter in most Protestant Churches. The emphasis is on the Lord Jesus Christ and usually stresses His suffering, surrender, devotion and death. It includes Palm Sunday, Maunday Thursday and Good Friday. Often times during Lent, such serial preaching about Jesus Christ leads application and emphasis of the Christian devotion, surrender, suffering, and allegiance to Jesus Christ.

B. Material for Lent

There is ample material for Gospel preaching with the lenten emphasis in Old Testament prophecy and the Gospel record of our Lord Jesus Christ. This material abounds in the emphasis and the sayings of our Lord and Saviour, Jesus Christ.

There are two extremes observed in Lent. Some are afraid to use Biblical lenten material because they are opposed to stressing the humanity of Christ. There are others who carry the extreme of emphasizing Christ's humanity forgetting His divinity, that is His divine sonship. The Bible reveals Christ as both human and divine in His earthly incarnation. Therefore, both His humanity and divinity can be emphasized and balanced in proper lenten serial preaching.

LENTEN QUESTIONS OF CONDUCT

1. Whom Do Men Say That I the Son of Man Am? Matt. 16: 13, "Whom do men say that I the Son of man am?"

2. Is It Lawful to Give Tribute to Caesar? Matt. 22: 17, "What thinkest thou? Is it lawful to give tribute unto Caesar, or not?"

3. Why Tempt Ye Me? Matt. 22: 18, "Why tempt ye me, ye hypocrites?"

4. Friend, Wherefore Art Thou Come? Matt. 26: 50, "Friend, wherefore art thou come?"

5. Lord, Is It I? Matt. 26: 22, "They were exceeding sorrowful, and began every one of them to say unto him, Lord, is it I?"

6. What Shall I Do Then With Jesus? Matt. 27: 22, "Pilate saith unto them, What then shall I do with Jesus which is called Christ?"

7. Who Shall Roll Us Away the Stone? Mark 16: 3, "And they said among themselves, Who shall roll us away the stone from the door of the sepulchre?"

LENTEN MUSTS

1. Christ Must Do the Father's Business. Luke 2: 49, "Wist ye not that I must be about my Father's business?"

2. Christ Must Suffer. Mark 8: 31, "And he began to teach them, that the Son of man must suffer many things, and be rejected of the elders."

3. Christ, Our Passover, Must be Killed. Luke 22: 7, "Then came the day of unleavened bread, when the passover must be killed."

4. Christ Must Needs Go through Samaria. John 4: 4, "And he must needs go through Samaria."

5. We Must Glory in Christ's Cross. I Cor. 11: 30, "For this cause many are weak and sickly among you, and many sleep."

6. Christ Must Reign. I Cor. 15: 25, "For he must reign, till he hath put all enemies under his feet."

CHRIST'S WORDS ON THE CROSS

1. The Prayer for His Enemies. Luke 23: 34, "Then said Jesus, Father, forgive them; for they know not what they do."

2. The Promise to the Repentant Robber. Luke 23: 43, "Jesus said unto him, Verily I say unto thee, To day shalt thou be with me in paradise."

3. The Charge to His Mother and to John. John 19: 26-27, "He saith unto his mother, Woman, behold thy son! Then saith he to the disciple, Behold thy mother."

4. The Cry of Desolation. Mark 15: 34, "My God, my God, why hast thou forsaken me?"

5. The Cry of Physical Anguish. John 19: 28, "After this, Jesus ... saith, I thirst."

6. The Cry of Victory. John 19: 30, "He said, It is finished: and he bowed his head, and gave up the ghost."

7. The Cry of Resignation. Luke 23: 46, "And when Jesus had cried with a loud voice, he said, Father, into thy hands I commend my spirit."

DOCTRINAL QUESTIONS OF LENT

1. Who Started Lent? John 3: 16, "For God so loved the world, that he gave his only begotten Son."

2. What Determined Christ's Course? Mark 10: 33, "Saying, Behold, we go up to Jerusalem; and the Son of man shall be delivered unto the chief priests."

3. Can We Suffer Vicariously for Others? Col. 1: 24, "Who now rejoice in my sufferings for you."

4. What Shall I do with Jesus? Matt. 27: 22, "Pilate saith unto them, What shall I do then with Jesus which is called Christ?"

5. Who Killed Jesus? Acts 2: 23, "Him, being delivered by the determinate counsel and foreknowledge of God."

LENT FOR MODERN LIFE

1. Grace for Lent. II Cor. 8: 9, "For ye know the grace of our Lord Jesus Christ."

2. Glory through Lent. John 1: 14, "And the Word was made flesh, and dwelt among us, and we beheld his glory."

3. Fellowship during Lent. Gal. 2: 20, "I am crucified with Christ: nevertheless I live; yet not I, but Christ liveth in me."

PASSION PERSONALITIES

1. The Leaven of Pharisees and Sadducees. Matt. 16: 6, "Then Jesus said unto them, Take heed and beware of the leaven of the Pharisees and of the Sadducees.

2. Judas, the Betrayer. Matt. 26: 48, "Now he that betrayed him gave them a sign, saying, Whomsoever I shall kiss, that same is he: hold him fast."

3. Sleeping Disciples. Matt. 26: 40, "What, could ye not watch with me one hour?"

4. Pilate, the Judged Judge. Matt. 27: 24, "I am innocent of the blood of this just person: see ye to it."

5. Peter, the Denier. Matt. 26: 72, "And again he denied with an oath, I do not know the man.

6. Ministering Women. Matt. 27: 55, "And many women were there beholding afar off."

7. Nicodemus, the Courageous. John 19: 39, "And there came also Nicodemus, which at first came to Jesus by night."

LENTEN PREDICTIONS IN ISAIAH 53

1. Believed Revelation. Vs. 1, "Who hath believed our report? and to whom is the arm of the Lord revealed?"

2. A Tender Plant. Vs. 2, "For he shall grow up before him as a tender plant, and as a root out of dry ground."

3. Despised and Rejected. Vs. 3, "He is despised and rejected of men; a man of sorrows, and acquainted with grief."

4. Wounded for Transgressions. Vs. 5, "But he was wounded for our transgressions, he was bruised for our iniquities."

5. Complete Submission. Vs. 7, "He was oppressed, and he was afflicted, yet he opened not his mouth."

6. Death and Burial. Vs. 9, "And he made his grave with the wicked, and with the rich in his death."

7. Victory Assured. Vs. 12, "Therefore will I divide him a portion with the great, and he shall divide the spoil with the strong."

GARDENS OF LENT

1. The Garden of Sin. Gen. 3: 15, "And I will put enmity between thee and the woman, and between thy seed and her seed."

2. The Garden of Temptation. Matt. 4: 1, "Then was Jesus led up of the spirit into the wilderness to be tempted of the devil."

3. The Garden of Agony. Matt. 26: 39, "And he went a little farther, and fell on his face, and prayed, saying, O my Father, if it be possible, let this cup pass from me: nevertheless not as I will, but as thou wilt."

4. The Garden of Burial. John 19: 41, "Now in the place where he was crucified there was a garden; and in the garden a new sepulchre, wherein was never man yet laid."

LENTEN BETWEENS

1. Between Two Committals. Luke 22: 42, "If thou be willing, remove this cup from me: nevertheless not my will, but thine, be done."

2. Between Two Kingdoms. Mark 11: 10, "Blessed be the kingdom of our father David, that cometh in the name of the Lord: Hosanna in the highest."

3. Between Two Bargains. Luke 22: 4, "He went his way, and communed with the chief priests and captains, how he might betray him unto them."

4. Between Two Decisions. Matt. 27: 21, "The governor answered and said unto them, Whether of the twain will ye that I release unto you? They said, Barabbas."

5. Between Two Criminals. Luke 23: 33, "There they crucified him, and the malefactors, one on the right hand, and the other on the left."

6. Between Two Worlds. Mark 15: 24, "And when they had crucified him, they parted his garments, casting lots upon them, what every man should take."

PERSONAL QUESTIONS OF LENT

1. To What Purpose This Waste? Matt. 26: 8, "When his disciples saw it, they had indignation, saying, "To what purpose is this waste?"

2. Lord is it I? Matt. 26: 22, "And they were exceeding sorrowful, and began every one of them to say unto him, Lord, is it I?"

3. Could Ye Not Watch With Me One Hour? Matt. 26: 40, "And saith unto Peter, What, could ye not watch with me one hour?"

4. Friend, Wherefore Art Thou Come? Matt. 26: 50, "And Jesus said unto him, Friend, wherefore art thou come?"

5. Whom Will Ye That I Release? Matt. 27: 17, "Pilate said unto them, Whom will ye that I release unto you? Barabbas, or Jesus which is called Christ?"

6. What Shall I Do Then with Jesus? Matt. 27: 22, "Pilate said unto them, What shall I do then with Jesus which is called Christ?"

7. Why Hast Thou Forsaken Me? Matt. 27: 46, "My God, my God, why hast thou forsaken me?"

LENTEN CONTRASTS

1. Christ and Barabbas. Matt. 27: 17, "Whom will ye that I release unto you? Barabbas, or Jesus which is called Christ?"

2. The Jews and the Gentiles. Matt. 27: 42, "He saved others; himself he cannot save. If he be the King of Israel, let him now come down from the cross, and we will believe him."

3. Pilate and Pilate's Wife. Matt. 27: 19, "When he was set down on the judgment seat, his wife sent unto him, saying, Have thou nothing to do with that just man."

4. Condemning and Confessing Robbers. Luke 23: 39, "And one of the malefactors which were hanged railed on him, saying, If thou be Christ, save thyself and us."

5. Peter and Nicodemus. John 18: 25, "And Simon Peter stood and warmed himself. . . . He denied it, and said, I am not."

LENTEN DECISIONS

1. Follow or Forsake. Matt. 26: 58, "But Peter followed him afar off unto the high priest's palace."

2. Fulfillment or Foolishness. Matt. 26: 56, "And all this was done, that the scriptures of the prophets might be fulfilled."

3. Condemn or Condone. Matt. 27: 17, "Pilate said unto them, Whom will ye that I release unto you? Barabbas, or Jesus which is called Christ?"

4. Blood of Redemption, or Blood of Retribution. Matt. 27: 25, "Then answered all the people, and said, His blood be on us, and on our children."

5. Weep for Yourselves or for Christ. Luke 23: 28, "Jesus turning unto them said, Daughters of Jerusalem, weep not for me, but weep for yourselves, and for your children."

6. Power or Perplexity. John 17: 1, "Father, the hour is come; glorify thy Son, that thy Son also may glorify thee."

DOCTRINE IN LENT

1. Christ's Humanity. Luke 2: 22, "They brought him to Jerusalem, to present him to the Lord."

2. Christ's Divinity. Matt. 26: 63, "I adjure thee by the living God, that thou tell us whether thou be the Christ, the Son of God."

3. Christ's Humility. Isa. 53: 2, "For he shall grow up before him as a tender plant, and as a root out of a dry ground."

1. The Bread of Life. John 6: 51, "I am the living bread which came down from heaven."

2. The Light of the World. John 8: 12, "I am the light of the world: he that followeth me shall not walk in darkness, but shall have the light of life."

3. The Light of Abraham. John 8: 58, "And Jesus said unto them, Verily, verily, I say unto you, Before Abraham was, I am."

4. The Way, Truth and Life. John 14: 6, "Jesus saith unto him, I am the way, the truth, and the life: no man cometh unto the Father, but by me."

5. The Messiah. John 4: 26, "Jesus saith unto her, I that speak unto thee am he."

6. The True Vine. John 15: 1, "I am the true vine, and my Father is the husbandman."

7. The Resurrection, John 11:25, "Jesus said unto her, I am the resurrection, and the life: he that believeth in me, though he were dead, yet shall he live."

Chapter VIII

EASTER SERIES

A. Emphasis

Easter should be properly emphasized. It stresses the resurrection of Christ from the dead and His subsequent appearances. The doctrine of the resurrection should have first place in all preaching as well as serial preaching on Easter. The resultant promise and guarantee of the Christian's resurrection and the Christian's victorious life because of the resurrection are also a part of the proper emphasis on Easter. It is possible therefore, to plan our present series of sermons on Easter truths for the benefit and blessing of all who hear.

B. Material for Easter

Old Testament prophecies and New Testament prophecies and predictions as well as the Gospel stories of Christ's resurrection furnish ample material for Easter Series. The Book of Acts commemorates the actual resurrection, the appearances of Christ and the resultant blessings of Christ's Easter victory. The effects of Easter are outlined in the Holy Scriptures and as ministers we do well to emphasize these truths. A large number of people believe that Christian life and Christ's life went with Easter. The Bible-believing Christian and the Bible-preaching minister should stress the effects and blessings of Easter through serial messages.

WHY JESUS DIED

1. For Sin. Heb. 9: 26, "For then must he often have suffered . . . for sin."

2. For the Unjust. I Peter 3: 18, "For Christ also hath once suffered for sins, the just for the unjust."

3. For Deliverance. Gal. 3: 13, "Christ hath redeemed us from the curse of the law."

4. For Reconciliation. II Cor. 5: 18-21. "God, who hath reconciled us to himself by Jesus Christ."

EASTER RESULTS

1. For Forgiveness. I Cor. 15: 3, "Christ died for our sins."

2. For Enlightenment. John 20: 29, "Thomas, because thou hast seen me, thou hast believed."

3. For Fellowship. Luke 24: 32, "Did not our heart burn within us, while he talked with us?"

4. For Appearance. Acts 9: 5, "I am Jesus whom thou persecutest."

5. For Victory. I Cor. 15: 57, "Thanks be to God, which giveth us the victory."

RESURRECTION REALITIES

1. Prophesied. John 11: 25, 26, "I am the resurrection, and the life. . . ."

2. Prescribed. John 10: 17, "I lay down my life, that I might take it again."

3. Procured. I Cor. 15: 22, ". . . in Christ shall all be made alive."

4. Proclaimed. I Cor. 15: 54, "Death is swallowed up in victory."

5. Practiced. I Cor. 15: 58, "Therefore . . . be ye stedfast, unmoveable. . . ."

EASTER DOCTRINES

1. The Resurrection of Christ. Matt. 28: 6, "He is not here: for he is risen, as he said."

2. The Resurrection of the Believer. I Cor. 15: 20, "But now is Christ risen . . . and become the firstfruits. . . ."

3. The Reign of Christ. I Cor. 15: 25, "For he must reign, till he hath put all enemies under his feet."

4. Life Eternal. John 17: 3, "This is life eternal, that they might know thee the only true God. . . ."

EASTER EFFECTS

1. On Believers. Rom. 6: 4, "That like as Christ was raised up from the dead by the glory of the Father, even so we also should walk in newness of life."

2. On Peter. Luke 24: 34, "Saying, The Lord is risen indeed, and hath appeared to Simon."

3. On the Guard. Matt. 28: 11, "Some of the watch came into the city, and shewed unto the chief priests all the things that were done."

4. On Sunday Walkers. Luke 24: 24, "And certain of them which were with us went to the sepulchre, and found it even so as the women had said."

5. On Doubting Thomas. John 20: 28, "And Thomas answered and said unto him, My Lord and my God."

6. On Sky Gazers. Acts 1: 4, "But wait for the promise of the Father, which, saith he, ye have heard of me."

7. On All Believers. John 11: 26, "And whosoever liveth and believeth in me shall never die."

EASTER MYSTERIES

1. Invisible Presence. John 20: 19, "Where the disciples were assembled . . . came Jesus and stood in the midst and saith unto them, Peace be unto you."

2. Invisible Peace. John 20: 21, "Then said Jesus to them again, Peace be unto you."

3. Invisible Persuasion. Luke 24: 31, "And their eyes were opened, and they knew him; and he vanished out of their sight."

4. Invisible Power. Col. 3: 3, "For ye are dead, and your life is hid with Christ in God.

EASTER QUESTIONS

1. Who Shall Roll Away the Stone? Mark 16: 3, "They said among themselves, Who shall roll us away the stone from the door of the sepulchre?"

2. Why Weepest Thou? John 20: 13, "And they say unto her, Woman, why weepest thou?"

3. Why Seek Ye the Living among the Dead? Luke 24: 5, "And they said unto them, Why seek ye the living among the dead?"

4. Why Disbelieve? Luke 24: 25, "Then he said unto them, O fools, and slow of heart to believe all that the prophets have spoken."

5. Why Doubt? John 20: 27, "Then saith he to Thomas, Reach hither thy finger, and behold my hands; and reach hither thy hand, and thrust it into my side: and be not faithless, but believing."

6. Lovest Thou Me? John 21: 15, "Simon Peter, Simon, son of Jonas, lovest thou me more than these?"

Chapter IX
ADVENT SERIES

A. Emphasis

The emphasis of Advent at most Protestant churches takes place on the fourth Sunday preceeding Christmas. Usually preparatory prophecies and persons involved in the early life of Christ are discussed and described in Advent series of sermons. Such sermonic emphasis can and should lead up to a proper observance of Christmas and the close of the Calendar year in December.

B. Material

The prophecies and preparation usually emphasised in Advent may be found in both the Old Testament and the New Testament. This Biblical material offers a greater appreciation for the preparation of Christ's coming and a new spiritual preparation for the people.

ADVENT PROPHECIES

1. Seed of the Woman. Gen. 3: 15, "And I will put enmity between thee and the woman, and between thy seed and her seed; it shall bruise thy head, and thou shalt bruise his heel."

2. Seed of Abraham. Matt. 1: 1, "The book of the generation of Jesus Christ, the son of David, the son of Abraham."

3. Promise Made to David. II Sam. 7: 12, "And when thy days be fulfilled, and thou shalt sleep with thy fathers, I will set up thy seed after thee."

4. His Coming and Kingdom. Mark 1: 15, "And saying, The time is fulfilled, and the kingdom of God is at hand: repent ye, and believe the gospel.

ADVENT WITNESSES

1. The Angels. Luke 2: 9, "And, lo, the angel of the Lord came upon them, and the glory of the Lord shone round about them."

2. The Shepherds. Luke 2: 17, "And when they had seen it, they made known abroad the saying which was told them concerning this child."

3. The Wise Men. Matt. 2: 2, "Saying, Where is he that is born King of the Jews? for we have seen his star in the east, and are come to worship him."

4. The Parents. Matt. 2: 14, "When he arose, he took the young child and his mother by night, and departed into Egypt."

ADVENT GROWTH

Advent Growth – Luke 2: 52, "And Jesus increased in wisdom and stature, and in favour with God and man.

1. Intellectually – Jesus Increased in Wisdom. Luke 2: 52.

2. Physically – Jesus Increased in Stature. Luke 2: 52.

3. Spiritually – Jesus Increased in Favour with God. Luke 2:52.

4. Morally – Jesus Increased in Favour with man. Luke 2:52.

ADVENT PREPARATION

1. The Birth of John the Baptist. Luke 1: 76, "For thou shalt go before the face of the Lord to prepare his ways."

2. The Voice of John. John 1: 23, "He said, I am the voice of one crying in the wilderness, Make straight the way of the Lord."

3. The Spirit of John. John 1: 37, "And the two disciples heard him speak, and they followed Jesus."

4. The Baptism of John. Matt. 3: 16, "And Jesus, when he was baptized, went up straightway out of the water."

ADVENT PREACHING

1. Prepare the Way. Luke 3: 4, "The voice of one crying in the wilderness, Prepare ye the way of the Lord, make his paths straight."

2. Repentance. Luke 3: 8, "Bring forth therefore fruits worthy of repentance."

3. Prepare Your Entire Life. Luke 3: 13, "And he said unto them, Exact no more than that which is appointed you."

4. Prepare for Spirit Baptism. Luke 3: 16, "But one mightier than I cometh, the latchet of whose shoes I am not worthy to unloose: he shall baptize you with the Holy Ghost and with fire."

ADVENT COMPARISONS

1. Greater Than John. Matt. 11: 11, "Verily I say unto you, Among them that are born of women there hath not risen a greater than John the Baptist."

2. Greater Than the Temple. Matt. 12: 6, "But I say unto you, That in this place is one greater than the temple."

3. Greater Than Jonas. Matt. 12: 41, "Behold, a greater than Jonas is here."

4. Greater Than Solomon. Matt. 12: 42, "Behold, a greater than Solomon is here."

5. Greater Than These Words. John 14: 12, "And greater works than these shall he do; because I go unto my Father."

ADVENT JOY

1. Complete Harmony. Isa. 9: 6, "The mighty God, The everlasting Father, The Prince of Peace."

2. Mary's Magnificat. Luke 1: 47, "And my spirit hath rejoiced in God my Saviour."

3. The Angelic Melody. Luke 2: 14, "Glory to God in the highest, and on earth peace, good will toward men."

4. And Many Shall Rejoice. Luke 1: 15, "For he shall be great in the sight of the Lord, and shall drink neither wine nor strong drink."

ADVENT ANNOUNCEMENTS

1. To Mary. Luke 1: 30, "And the angel said unto her, Fear not, Mary: for thou hast found favor with God."

2. To Joseph. Matt. 1: 20, "The angel of the Lord appeared unto him in a dream, saying, Joseph, thou son of David, fear not to take unto thee Mary thy wife."

3. To the Shepherds. Luke 2: 10, "And the angel said unto them, Fear not: for, behold, I bring you good tidings of great joy, which shall be to all people."

4. To Simeon. Luke 2: 26, "And it was revealed unto him by the Holy Ghost, that he should not see death, before he had seen the Lord's Christ."

5. To the Magi. Matt. 2: 10, "When they saw the star, they rejoiced with exceeding great joy."

ADVENT NAMES

1. The Name Jesus. Matt. 1: 21, "Thou shalt call his name Jesus: for he shall save his people from their sins."

2. The Name Immanuel. Matt. 1: 23, "They shall call his name Immanuel, which being interpreted is, God with us."

3. The Name Christ the Lord. Luke 2: 11, "For unto you is born this day in the city of David a Savior, which is Christ the Lord."

4. The Name the Nazarene. Matt. 2: 23, "He shall be called a Nazarene."

ADVENT PREPARATIONS

1. Room in Your Heart. Luke 2: 7, "And laid him in a manger; because there was no room for them in the inn."

2. Prepare the Way. Isa. 40: 3, "Prepare ye the way of the Lord, make straight in the desert a highway for our God."

3. Looking for Consolation. Luke 2: 25, "Waiting for the consolation of Israel: and the Holy Ghost was upon him."

4. Following the Star. Matt. 2: 4, "He demanded of them where Christ should be born."

ADVENT REVELATION

1. Beginning of the Word. John 1: 1, "In the beginning was the Word, and the Word was with God, and the Word was God."

2. Beginning of Light. John 1: 7, "The same came for a witness, to bear witness of the Light, that all men through him might believe."

3. Beginning of Salvation. John 1: 2, "The same was in the beginning with God."

4. Beginning of Grace and Truth. John 1: 17, "For the law was given by Moses, but grace and truth came by Jesus Christ."

ADVENT IN SONG

1. Glory. Ps. 72: 19, "And blessed be his glorious name forever: and let the whole earth be filled with his glory."

2. Mercy. Ps. 89: 1, "I will sing of the mercies of the Lord for ever."

3. Hope. Ps. 130: 7, "Let Israel hope in the Lord: for with the Lord there is mercy, and with him is plenteous redemption."

4. Righteousness. Jer. 23: 5, "Behold, the days come, saith the Lord, that I will raise unto David a righteous Branch."

ADVENT PERSONALITIES

1. Zacharias and Elizabeth. Luke 1: 6, "And they were both righteous before God, walking in all the commandments and ordinances of the Lord blameless."

2. Mary and Joseph. Luke 1: 27, "To a virgin espoused to a man whose name was Joseph, of the house of David; and the virgin's name was Mary."

3. Simeon. Luke 2: 25, "And behold, there was a man in Jerusalem, whose name was Simeon; and the same man was just and devout, waiting for the consolation of Israel."

4. The Magi. Matt. 2: 1, "Behold, there came wise men from the east to Jerusalem."

ADVENT PURPOSES

1. Cultivate Peace. Matt. 5: 9, "Blessed are the peacemakers: for they shall be called the children of God."

2. Show Good Will. Heb. 13: 21, "Make you perfect in every good work to do his will."

3. Demonstrate Love. Matt. 2: 11, "And when they had opened their treasures, they presented unto him gifts; gold, and frankincense, and myrrh."

4. Spread Joy. Acts 8: 8, "And there was great joy in that city."

SPIRITUAL ADVENT

1. Follow the Star. Matt. 2: 2, "Saying, Where is he that is born King of the Jews? for we have seen his star in the east, and are come to worship him."

2. Give Good Gifts. Matt. 2: 11, "And when they had opened their treasures, they presented unto him gifts; gold, and frankincense, and myrrh."

3. God's Sacrifice. Phil. 2: 7, "But made himself of no reputation, and took upon him the form of a servant, and was made in the likeness of men."

4. Christ in Us. Gal. 4: 19, "Until Christ be formed in you."

ADVENT GIFTS

1. The Gift Given. Luke 2: 6, "And so it was, that, while they were there, the days were accomplished that she should be delivered."

2. The Gift Described. Luke 2: 11, "For unto you is born this day in the city of David a Savior, which is Christ the Lord."

3. The Gift Proclaimed. Luke 2: 17, "And when they had seen it, they made known abroad the saying which was told them concerning this cnild."

4. The Gift Rejected. Luke 23: 21, "But they cried, saying, Crucify him, crucify him."

5. The Gift Received. John 3: 36, "He that believeth on the Son hath everlasting life."

ADVENT SONGS

1. The Song of His Mother. Luke 1: 46, 47, "And Mary said, My soul doth magnify the Lord, and my spirit hath rejoiced in God my Savior."

2. The Song of Elizabeth. Luke 1: 42, "And she spake out with a loud voice, and said, Blessed art thou among women."

3. The Song of the Angels. Luke 2: 10, "And the angel said unto them, Fear not: for, behold, I bring you good tidings of great joy, which shall be to all people."

4. The Song of the Prophet. Luke 2: 34, "And Simeon blessed them, and said unto Mary his mother, Behold, this child is set for the fall and rising again of many in Israel."

Chapter X
BIBLE CHARACTER SERIES

Bible biographical sermons in series can be very interesting both for the minister and his people. If properly prepared such sermons will touch life at many points because Bible characters were much like we are, troubled, tempted, tested and sometimes triumphant. Such series will be intensely practical not only because of human interest on the part of the listener but also because of common experience and expression. Such a series must represent a popular treatment of the facts of Bible characters related to life and experience as we find it today. Such a series will include doctrine and the application of personal as well as social ethics in every day living.

Two kinds of series may be observed. One series in type will represent several characters in one part of the Bible, in one book of the Bible, associated with some special events in the Bible or leading up to a climax as we find it in the life of our Lord Jesus Christ.

Another type of biographical sermon series can be several biographical sermons on the same character. As the later part of this chapter will show, beautiful series can be formulated on single characters with variety of passages and lessons to be observed.

In preaching a biographical sermon whether to cover the entire character in one sermon, or to present part of one character in a series devoted to that character there are two methods of preparation and presentation which prevail. One type of method involves the preparation and the telling of the selected portion or portions of biographical material for the first point of the sermon and the second division of the sermon is devoted to the application of material of first division in the second division. The other method of biographical sermon is to make each division use some part of the biographical material together with an application or deduction of such material. It is well to vary the method. This is good training for the minister and makes for good variety for his people.

The chapter heading reads correctly Bible Character Series

and excludes other character series. Some ministers like to use character studies from our political, our literary, our industrial history and present historical sermons on these men. Even ministers have been used as subjects for biographical sermon series. Again, we are reminded that God's blessing rests on the spoken word about His Word and not on the words or lives of men. There is no excuse for using character study of individuals other than those found in the Scripture. The minister is duty bound to use only Bible characters in this type of series. The Scriptures abound with examples, full of interesting sermonic material for up-to-date practical modern living. Just taking a secular character and hinging his life on a text by a thin thread as an excuse for a Bible biographical sermon is inexcusable and should not be tolerated. Interesting data from secular characters, particularly if they were or are Christian, can be used as fine illustrative material in sermons that are based squarely on the Word of God. Such material may only be used as secondary source and as illustrative material to give outside light or contrast on the Word of Life found in the Bible.

There are dangers in biographical sermons. Often the long contextual introductions spoil interest and instruction. Keep such sermons close to their Bible context but also close to modern day living with proper spiritual and psychological bearing and blessing.

COMPANIONS IN SERVICE

1. Moses and Aaron. Ex. 7: 1, "And the Lord said unto Moses, See, I have made thee a god to Pharaoh: and Aaron thy brother shall be thy prophet."

2. Abraham and Isaac. Gen. 22: 3, "And Abraham rose up early in the morning... and took two of his young men with him, and Isaac his son."

3. David and Jonathan. I Sam. 18: 1, "The soul of Jonathan was knit with the soul of David, and Jonathan loved him as his own soul."

4. Elisabeth and Mary. Luke 1: 41, "And it came to pass, that, when Elisabeth heard the salutation of Mary, the babe

leaped in her womb; and Elisabeth was filled with the Holy Ghost."

5. Jesus and Disciples. John 15: 14, "Ye are my friends, if ye do whatsoever I command you."

6. Paul and Barnabas. Acts 15: 22, "To send chosen men of their own company to Antioch with Paul and Barnabas."

ALTAR BUILDERS

1. Noah. Gen. 8: 20, "And Noah builded an altar unto the Lord."

2. Abraham. Gen. 12: 8, "And there he builded an altar unto the Lord, and called upon the name of the Lord."

3. Moses. Ex. 17: 15, "And Moses built an altar."

4. Saul. I Sam. 14: 35, "And Saul built an altar unto the Lord: the same was the first altar that he built unto the Lord."

5. Elijah. I Kings 18: 30, "And he repaired the altar of the Lord that was broken down."

6. Solomon. II Chron. 4: 1, "Moreover he made an altar of brass, twenty cubits the length thereof."

DEEDS OF KINDNESS

1. A Maiden's Message. II Kings 5: 3, "Would God my lord were with the prophet that is in Samaria! for he would recover him of his leprosy."

2. The Good Samaritan. Luke 10: 33, "But a certain Samaritan, as he journeyed, came where he was: and when he saw him, he had compassion on him."

3. The Warning of Pilate's Wife. Matt. 27: 19, "His wife sent unto him, saying, Have thou nothing to do with that just man."

4. Eutychus Restored. Acts 20: 9-12, "And there sat in the window a certain young man named Eutychus, being fallen into a deep sleep . . . . "

5. A Nephew's Secret. Acts 23: 16, "And when Paul's sister's son heard of their lying in wait, he went and entered into the castle, and told Paul."

MEN WHO WALKED WITH GOD

1. Enoch. Gen. 5: 24, "And Enoch walked with God: and he was not; for God took him."

2. Noah. Gen. 6: 9, "Noah was a just man and perfect in his generations, and Noah walked with God."

3. Abraham. Gen. 17: 1, "The Lord appeared to Abram, and said unto him, I am the Almighty God; walk before me, and be thou perfect."

4. Paul. Gal. 2: 20, "The life which I now live in the flesh I live by the faith of the Son of God."

5. Jesus. John 17: 21, "That they all may be one; as thou, Father, art in me, and I in thee."

AFFIRMATIONS OF ASSURANCE

1. Job in Sorrow. Job 1:21, "The Lord gave, and the Lord hath taken away; blessed be the name of the Lord."

2. Joshua in Decision. Josh. 24: 15, "But as for me and my house, we will serve the Lord."

3. David in Sin. Ps. 51: 3, "For I acknowledge my transgressions: and my sin is ever before me."

4. Peter in Reconsecration. John 21: 5, "Then Jesus saith unto them, Children, have ye any meat? They answered him, No."

5. Thomas in Confirmation. John 20: 28, "And Thomas answered and said unto him, My Lord and my God."

6. Mary in Praise. Luke 1: 46, "And Mary said, My soul doth magnify the Lord."

7. Jesus in Victory. John 10: 17, "Therefore doth my Father love me, because I lay down my life, that I might take it again."

8. Paul in Service. I Cor. 15: 58, "Be ye stedfast, unmoveable, always abounding in the work of the Lord."

PECULIAR CHARACTERS

1. A Good Mother-in-Law. Ruth 1: 12, "Turn again, my daughters, go your way."

2. A Spoiled Baby. I Kings 21: 4, "He laid him down upon his bed, and turned away his face, and would eat no bread."

3. An Adopted Daughter. Esther 2: 7, "And he brought up Hadassah, that is, Esther, his uncle's daughter: for she had neither father nor mother."

4. A Foolish Farmer. Luke 12: 20, "But God said unto him, Thou fool, this night thy soul shall be required of thee."

UNFAMILIAR FRIENDS OF PAUL

1. Priscilla and Aquila. Acts 18: 2, "And found a certain Jew named Aquila... with his wife Priscilla."

2. Phebe. Rom. 16: 1, "I commend unto you Phebe our sister, which is a servant of the church."

3. Clement. Phil. 4: 3, "With Clement also, and with other my fellowlabourers."

4. Onesimus. Philem. 10, "I beseech thee for my son Onesimus, whom I have begotten in my bonds."

5. Julius. Acts 27: 1, "And certain other prisoners unto one named Julius a centurion...."

EARLY RISERS

1. Abraham - To Sacrifice. Gen. 22: 3, "And Abraham rose up early in the morning... and went unto the place of which God had told him."

2. Jacob - To Worship. Gen. 28: 18, "And Jacob rose up early in the morning, and took the stone that he had put for his pillows, and set it up for a pillar, and poured oil upon the top of it."

3. Moses - To Ambassador. Ex. 8: 20, "And the Lord said unto Moses, Rise up early in the morning, and stand before Pharaoh."

4. Joshua - To Capture. Josh. 6: 12, "And Joshua rose early in the morning, and the priests took up the ark of the Lord."

5. Gideon - To Examine. Judg. 6:38, "For he rose up early on the morrow, and thrust the fleece together."

6. Jesus - To Pray. John 8: 2, "And early in the morning he came again into the temple, and all the people came unto him."

7. The People - To Hear. Luke 21: 38, "And all the people came early in the morning to him in the temple, for to hear him."

THEMES OF GREAT PREACHERS

1. Noah, Judgment. Heb. 11: 7, "By faith Noah, being warned of God of things not seen as yet, moved with fear, prepared an ark to the saving of his house."

2. Joseph, Evil. Gen. 37: 2, "Joseph, being seventeen years old, was feeding the flock with his brethren; and the lad was with the sons of Bilhah....and Joseph brought unto his father their evil report."

3. Moses, Deliverence. Ex. 8: 1, "And the Lord spake unto Moses, Go unto Pharaoh, and say unto him, Thus saith the Lord, Let my people go, that they may serve me."

4. Nathan, Sin. II Sam. 12: 7, "And Nathan said to David, Thou art the man."

5. John the Baptist, Repentance. Matt. 3: 8, "Bring forth therefore fruits meet for repentance."

6. Peter, Salvation. Acts 4: 12, "Neither is there salvation in any other: for there is none other name under heaven given among men, whereby we must be saved."

7. Paul, Service. Rom. 12: 1, "I beseech you therefore, brethren, by the mercies of God, that ye present your bodies a living sacrifice, holy, acceptable unto God, which is your reasonable service."

MOSES, THE LAWGIVER

1. Home Training. Ex. 2: 9, "And Pharaoh's daughter said unto her, Take this child away, and nurse it for me, and I will give thee thy wages."

2. Educational Training. Acts 7: 22, "And Moses was learned in all the wisdom of the Egyptians, and was mighty in words and in deeds."

3. Spiritual Training. Ex. 3:5, "And he said, Draw not nigh hither: put off thy shoes from off thy feet, for the place whereon thou standest is holy ground."

4. Leadership Service. Ex. 4: 28, "And Moses told Aaron all the words of the Lord who had sent him, and all the signs which he had commanded him."

5. Evidence before the Ungodly. Ex. 5: 1, "And afterward Moses and Aaron went in, and told Pharaoh, Thus saith the Lord God of Israel."

6. Blessings to God's People. Ex. 15: 22, "So Moses brought Israel from the Red sea, and they went out into the wilderness of Shur."

PETER, THE FORCEFUL

1. Conversion. John 1: 42, "Thou art Simon the son of Jona: thou shalt be called Cephas, which is by interpretation, A stone."

2. Call. Mark 1: 17, "And Jesus said unto them, Come ye after me, and I will make you to become fishers of men."

3. Confession. Matt. 16: 16, "And Simon Peter answered and said, Thou art the Christ, the Son of the living God."

4. Consecration. Matt. 26: 72, "And again he denied with an oath, I do not know the man."

5. Confirmed. I Cor. 15: 5, "And that he was seen of Cephas, then of the twelve."

6. Commitment. John 21: 17, "He saith unto him the third time, Simon, son of Jonas, lovest thou me?"

7. Conclusion. I Peter 1: 1, "Peter, an apostle of Jesus Christ."

CHARACTERISTICS OF JOHN THE BAPTIST

1. A Prophet. Matt. 11: 9, "What went ye out for to see? A prophet? yea, I say unto you, and more than a prophet."

2. A Bright Lamp. John 5: 35, "He was a burning and a shining light: and ye were willing for a season to rejoice in his light."

3. Paradox of Greatness. Matt. 11: 11, "Among them that are born of women there hath not risen a greater than John the Baptist."

4. Forerunner of Jesus. Matt. 11: 10, "For this is he, of whom it is written, Behold, I send my messenger before thy face, which shall prepare thy way before thee."

ELIJAH, THE TISHBITE

1. Appearance. II Kings 1: 8, "And he said, It is Elijah the Tishbite."

2. Message. I Kings 17: 1, "As the Lord God of Israel liveth, before whom I stand, there shall not be dew nor rain these years, but according to my word."

3. Nourished by Ravens. I Kings 17: 6, "And the ravens brought him bread and flesh in the morning, and bread and flesh in the evening."

4. Restores a Son. I Kings 17: 22, "And the Lord heard the voice of Elijah; and the soul of the child came into him again, and he revived."

5. Meets Ahab. I Kings 18: 18, "And he answered, I have not troubled Israel; but thou, and thy father's house."

6. Builds an Altar. I Kings 18: 30, "And he repaired the altar of the Lord that was broken down."

7. Life Threatened. I Kings 19: 2, "Then Jezebel sent a messenger unto Elijah, saying, So let the gods do to me, and more also, if I make not thy life as the life of one of them by tomorrow about this time."

8. Dejection under a Tree. I Kings 19: 4, "And sat down under a juniper tree: and he requested for himself that he might die."

9. His Successor. I Kings 19: 19, "So he departed thence, and found Elisha."

10. His Ascension. II Kings 2: 8, "And Elijah took his mantle, and wrapped it together, and smote the waters."

DAVID

1. A Beautiful Boy. I Sam. 17: 12, "Now David was the son of that Ephrathite of Bethlehem-judah, whose name was Jesse."

2. Chosen of the Lord. I Sam. 16: 1, "Fill thine horn with oil, and go, I will send thee to Jesse the Bethlehemite: for I have provided me a king among his sons."

3. Anointed by Samuel. I Sam. 16: 13, "Then Samuel took the horn of oil, and anointed him in the midst of his brethren."

4. Soothed Saul. I Sam. 16: 23, "David took an harp, and played with his hand: so Saul was refreshed, and was well."

5. Slays Goliath. I Sam. 17: 50, "So David prevailed over the Philistine with a sling and with a stone."

6. Enmity of Saul. I Sam. 18: 29, "And Saul was yet the more afraid of David; and Saul became David's enemy continually."

7. Jonathan Loves David. I Sam. 18: 1, "The soul of Jonathan was knit with the soul of David, and Jonathan loved him as his own soul."

8. An Outlaw Because of Saul. I Sam. 21: 10, "And David arose, and fled that day for fear of Saul."

9. David Spares Saul's Life. I Sam. 24: 7, "So David stayed his servants with these words, and suffered them not to rise against Saul."

10. David, King of Judah. II Sam. 2: 11, "And the time that David was king in Hebron over the house of Judah was seven years and six months."

11. David, God's Choice. II Sam. 7: 9, "And I was with thee whithersoever thou wentest, and have cut off all thine enemies out of thy sight."

CRISIS WITH A CHANGE OF NAME

1. Abram Becomes Abraham. Gen. 17: 5, "Neither shall thy name any more be called Abram, but thy name shall be Abraham."

2. Jacob Becomes Israel. Gen. 32: 28, "Thy name shall be called no more Jacob, but Israel."

3. Joseph Becomes Zaphnathpaaneah. Gen. 41: 45, "And Pharaoh called Joseph's name Zaphnathpaaneah."

4. Pashur Becomes Magormissabib. Jer. 20: 3, "Then said Jeremiah unto him, The Lord hath not called thy name Pashur but Magormissabib."

5. Daniel Becomes Belteshazzar. Dan. 1: 7, "For he gave unto Daniel the name of Belteshazzar."

6. Simon Peter Becomes Cephas. John 1: 42, "Thou art Simon the son of Jona: thou shalt be called Cephas, which is by interpretation, A stone."

7. Saul Becomes Paul. Acts 13: 9, "Then Saul, (who also is called Paul,) filled with the Holy Ghost, set his eyes on him."

PROFESSIONS OF THE BIBLE

1. Moses, The Lawgiver. Ex. 5: 1, "Thus saith the Lord God of Israel, Let my people go, that they may hold a feast unto me in the wilderness."

2. Joseph, The Prime Minister. Gen. 41: 41, "And Pharaoh said unto Joseph, See, I have set thee over all the land of Egypt."

3. Gamaliel, The Lawyer. Acts 5: 34, "Then stood there up one in the council, a Pharisee, named Gamaliel, a doctor of the law."

4. John, The Preacher. John 1: 29, "The next day John seeth Jesus coming unto him, and saith, Behold the Lamb of God, which taketh away the sin of the world."

5. Matthew, The Tax Collector. Matt. 9: 9, "And as Jesus passed forth from thence, he saw a man, named Matthew, sitting at the receipt of custom."

6. Paul, The Missionary. Acts 9: 15, "But the Lord said unto him, Go thy way: for he is a chosen vessel unto me."

7. Luke, The Physician. Col. 4: 14, "Luke, the beloved physician, and Demas, greet you."

8. Herod, The Governor. Matt. 14: 1, "At that time Herod the tetrarch heard of the fame of Jesus."

9. Jesus, the King. I Tim. 6: 15, "Which in his times he shall shew, who is the blessed and only Potentate, the King of kings, and Lord of lords."

ENEMY CHARACTERS OF THE NEW TESTAMENT

1. Hymenaeus and Philetus, Overthrowers of the Faith. II Tim. 2: 17, "And their word will eat as doth a canker: of whom is Hymenaeus and Philetus."

2. Phygellus and Hermogenes, Deserters of the Faith. II Tim. 1: 15, "This thou knowest, that all they which are in Asia be turned away from me; of whom are Phygellus and Hermogenes."

3. Jannes and Jambres, Resisters of the Faith. II Tim. 3: 8, "Now as Jannes and Jambres withstood Moses, so do these also resist the truth."

4. Demas, Forsaking the Faith. II Tim. 4: 10, "For Demas hath forsaken me, having loved this present world."

5. Alexander the Coppersmith, Damages the Faith. II Tim. 4: 14, "Alexander the coppersmith did me much evil."

6. Diotrephes, Self Preference to Faith. III John 9, "But Diotrephes, who loveth to have the preeminence among them, receiveth us not."

GOD'S MINUTE MEN

1. Moses Before Pharaoh. Ex. 5: 1, "And afterward Moses and Aaron went in, and told Pharaoh, Thus saith the Lord God of Israel."

2. Elijah Before Ahab. I Kings 18: 18, "And he answered, I have not troubled Israel; but thou, and thy father's house."

3. Nehemiah Before Artaxerxes. Neh. 2: 3, "And he said unto the king, Let the king live for ever: why should not my countenance be sad, when the city, the place of my fathers' sepulchres, lieth waste."

4. John the Baptist Before Herod. Matt. 14: 4, "For John said unto him, It is not lawful for thee to have her."

5. Christ Before Pilate. Matt. 27: 11, "And Jesus stood before the governor."

6. Paul Before Annas and Caiaphas. Acts 4: 8, "Then Peter, filled with the Holy Ghost, said unto them, Ye rulers of the people, and elders of Israel."

7. Paul Before Agrippa. Acts 26: 1, "Then Agrippa said unto Paul, Thou art permitted to speak for thyself."

ABRAHAM

1. Exalted Father. Gen. 17: 5, "Neither shall thy name any more be called Abram, but thy name shall be Abraham; for a father of many nations have I made thee."

2. Builds an Altar. Gen. 12: 7, "And there builded he an altar unto the Lord, who appeared unto him."

3. Separation from Lot. Gen. 13: 12, "Abram dwelled in the land of Canaan, and Lot dwelled in the cities of the plain."

4. Blessed by Melchizedek. Gen. 14: 19, "And he blessed him, and said, Blessed be Abram of the most high God, possessor of heaven and earth."

5. Believed God. Gen. 15: 6, "And he believed in the Lord; and he counted it to him for righteousness."

6. Visit of Angels. Gen. 18: 2, "And he lift up his eyes and looked, and, lo, three men stood by him."

7. Offers Isaac. Gen. 22: 13, "And Abraham lifted up his eyes, and looked, and behold behind him a ram caught in a thicket by his horns."

8. Death. Gen. 25: 8, "Then Abraham gave up the ghost, and died in a good old age, an old man, and full of years."

HEROES OF HEBREWS 11

1. Abel's Offering. Vs. 4, "By faith Abel offered unto God a more excellent sacrifice than Cain."

2. Enoch Pleased God. Vs. 5, "By faith Enoch was translated that he should not see death."

3. Noah Built the Ark. Vs. 7, "By faith Noah, being warned of God of things not seen as yet, moved with fear, prepared an ark to the saving of his house."

4. Abraham Obeyed God. Vs. 8, "By faith Abraham, when he was called to go out into a place which he should after receive for an inheritance, obeyed."

5. Sarah's Faith. Vs. 11, "Through faith also Sara herself received strength to conceive seed."

6. Isaac's Blessing. Vs. 20, "By faith Isaac blessed Jacob and Esau concerning things to come."

7. Jacob's Worship. Vs. 21, "By faith Jacob, when he was dying, blessed both the sons of Joseph."

8. Joseph's Prediction. Vs. 22, "By faith Joseph, when he died, made mention of the departing of the children of Israel."

9. Moses' Choice. Vs. 24, "By faith Moses, when he was come to years, refused to be called the son of Pharaoh's daughter."

10. Rahab Believed. Vs. 31, "By faith the harlot Rahab perished not with them that believed not."

DOUBLE CHARACTERS

1. A Successful Failure. Judg. 16: 28, "And Samson called unto the Lord . . . I pray thee, only this once, O God, that I may be at once avenged of the Philistines for my two eyes."

2. A Needy Powerful God. Mark 11: 3, "And if any man say unto you, Why do ye this? say ye that the Lord hath need of him; and straightway he will send him hither."

3. A Dead Living Woman. I Tim. 5: 6, "But she that liveth in pleasure is dead while she liveth."

4. A Devilish Disciple. John 6: 70, "Jesus answered them, Have not I chosen you twelve, and one of you is a devil?"

5. A Poor Rich Preacher. II Cor. 6: 10, "As poor, yet making many rich; as having nothing, and yet possessing all things."

Chapter XI

CHURCH HISTORY SERIES

The field of Church History is replete with sermonic illustration to be used in serial preaching. This field also lends itself to character studies which might seem profitable for sermonic serial preaching. As stated in the chapter on Bible Character Series, this author believes that sermons and series of sermons may only be preached on the basis of the Word of God. All other sources, even Church History, must be considered secondary and used only as illustrative material.

Because characters in the field of Church History represent so much Christian truth it may be possible to prepare series of sermons of Bible tests, and feature Church History Characters very largely as illustrations of that particular Biblical truth expounded. In this chapter such series will be suggested but in doing so, let it be remembered that the message is based on the Word and the historical references are for purposes of illustration and clarification only.

Some people idolize their historical heritage and great leaders found in such history. They exalt Church leaders, denominational figures and great missionaries. All of these can and should be used as illustrative material, but never be used singly and by themselves as a substitute for Biblical spiritual messages.

DOCTRINE AND DUTY

1. Dogmatic Doctrine. Rom. 12: 18, "If it be possible, as much as lieth in you, live peaceably with all men."

2. Diversity of Doctrine. Rom. 14: 19, "Let us therefore follow after the things which make for peace, and things wherewith one may edify another."

3. Christ-Centered Doctrine. John 1: 12, "But as many as received him, to them gave he power to become the sons of God."

4. Balanced Doctrine. II Tim. 2: 15, "Rightly dividing the word of truth."

GROWTH OF THE CHURCH

1. A United Front. Acts 2: 1, "And when the day of Pentecost was fully come, they were all with one accord in one place."

2. Martyr's Blood. Acts 8: 4. "Therefore they that were scattered abroad went every where preaching the word."

3. Blessing of God. Acts 2: 47, "And the Lord added to the church daily such as should be saved."

4. Spiritual Gospel. John 12: 32, "And I, if I be lifted up from the earth, will draw all men unto me."

REFORMATION REALITIES

1. Return of Apostolic Truth. Acts 2: 42, "And they continued stedfastly in the apostles' doctrine and fellowship, and in breaking of bread, and in prayers."

2. Return of God's Grace in Experience. Acts 9: 29, "And he spake boldly in the name of the Lord Jesus."

3. Return of Spiritual Tolerance. I Cor. 13: 1, "Though I speak with the tongues of men and of angels, and have not charity, I am become as sounding brass, or a tinkling cymbal."

4. Return of Spiritual Love. I Cor. 13: 3b, "And have not charity, it profiteth me nothing."

CHURCH PROGRAM LESSONS

1. Spiritual, Not Hierarchical Methods. Zech. 4: 6, "Not by might, nor by power, but by my spirit, saith the Lord of hosts."

2. Spiritual Accommodation. Heb. 13: 5, "Let your conversation be without covetousness; and be content with such things as ye have."

3. Spiritual Goal. Heb. 12: 1, "Let us lay aside every weight, and the sin which doth so easily beset us, and let us run with patience the race that is set before us."

4. Spiritual Action. Col. 3: 13, "Forbearing one another, and forgiving one another."

CHRIST FOR THE CRISIS

1. Christ is Central, Not Pope or Potentate. John 14: 6, "Jesus saith unto him, I am the way, the truth, and the life: no man cometh unto the Father, but by me."

2. Christ is Revelation, Not Tradition or Fancy. Heb. 1: 2, "Hath in these last days spoken unto us by his Son."

3. Christ is Foundational, Not Decretals or Decrees. I Cor. 3: 11, "For other foundation can no man lay than that is laid, which is Jesus Christ."

4. Christ is Eternal Life, Not in the Church or Man's Promise. John 17: 3, "And this is life eternal, that they might know thee the only true God, and Jesus Christ, whom thou hast sent."

TRUTH BREAKS TRADITION

1. Truth Brings Freedom (Not free in closed church). John 8: 32, "And ye shall know the truth, and the truth shall make you free."

2. Truth Brings Life (Not tradition first). John 14: 6, "Jesus saith unto him, I am the way, the truth, and the life: no man cometh unto the Father, but by me."

3. Truth Brings Interpretation (Sometimes heresy stimulates it). II Tim. 2: 15, "Rightly dividing the word of truth."

4. Truth Brings Spirit Guidance (Power of Pentecost). John 16: 13, "Howbeit when he, the Spirit of truth, is come, he will guide you into all truth."

FULLNESS OF TIME

1. Appearance of Christ (Inter-Testamentary Times). Gal. 4: 4, "But when the fulness of time was come, God sent forth his Son, made of a woman, made under the law."

2. Antecedents of Events (Preparatory factor in History).
   I Cor. 3: 6, "I have planted, Apollos watered; but God gave
   the increase."

3. Appraisal of Justice (Justice has always triumphed in the
   end). Acts 17: 31, "Because he hath appointed a day, in the
   which he will judge the world in righteousness."

4. Approval of the Bible (The return to the Bible marks its approval). Rom. 10: 17, "So then faith cometh by hearing, and
   hearing by the word of God."

5. Application of the Holy Spirit (The Holy Spirit has been active
   in history). John 16: 13, "Howbeit when he, the Spirit of
   truth, is come, he will guide you into all truth."

OPPOSITION TO THE CHURCH

1. Physical Opposition (Early persecution in the Church).
   Acts 4: 3, "And they laid hands on them, and put them in
   hold unto the next day."

2. Intellectual Opposition (Pagan philosophers fought the faith).
   I Cor. 3: 19, "For the wisdom of this world is foolishness
   with God."

3. Satanic Opposition (Satan has gone parallel to God to destroy).
   Luke 22: 31, "And the Lord said, Simon, Simon, behold,
   Satan hath desired to have you, that he may sift you as wheat."

4. Secular Opposition (Present day secularism). II Tim. 3: 1,
   "This know also, that in the last days perilous times shall
   come."

BIBLE BLESSINGS

1. Greater Than Philosophies (Period of Illumination). I Cor.
   2: 3, "And I was with you in weakness, and in fear, and in
   much trembling."

2. Greater Than Formal Worship (Hildebrandian Age). II Tim.
   4: 2, "Preach the word . . . exhort with all longsuffering
   and doctrine."

3. Greater Than Heresy (Reformation Period). John 1: 1, "In the beginning was the Word, and the Word was with God, and the Word was God."

4. Greater Than Man's Word (Imperial Age). I Peter 1: 25, "But the word of the Lord endureth for ever."

WEAKNESSES OF PROTESTANTISM

1. Weak Theological Emphasis. John 8: 32, "And ye shall know the truth, and the truth shall make you free."

2. Living for the World. I John 2: 15, "Love not the world, neither the things that are in the world."

3. Poor Conception of the Church. Col. 1: 18, "And he is the head of the body, the church."

4. Poor Evangelism. Acts 1: 8, "And ye shall be witnesses unto me both in Jerusalem, and in all Judaea, and in Samaria, and unto the uttermost part of the earth."

5. Weak Educational Training. Prov. 22: 6, "Train up a child in the way he should go: and when he is old, he will not depart from it."

6. Self Complacency. Amos 6: 1, "Woe to them that are at ease in Zion."

7. Flimsy Social Consciousness. Luke 10: 33, "And when he saw him, he had compassion on him."

8. Weak Personal Living Faith. Luke 17: 5, "And the apostles said unto the Lord, Increase our faith."

FUNCTIONS OF THE CHURCH

1. Live by the Scriptures (Not the traditions only). Ps. 119: 105, "Thy word is a lamp unto my feet, and a light unto my path."

2. True to Christ (Not to earthly leaders first and only). Col. 1: 18, "And he is the head of the body, the church."

3. Ministerial Discipline (Not hierarchical). Matt. 18: 17, "And if he shall neglect to hear them, tell it unto the church."

4. Biblical Missions (Not for power and prestige). Matt. 28: 19, "Go ye therefore, and teach all nations, baptizing them in the name of the Father, and of the Son, and of the Holy Ghost."

DANGERS OF THE CHURCH

1. Formalism Means Decline. Jer. 6: 20, "To what purpose cometh there to me incense from Sheba, and the sweet cane from a far country?"

2. Force Eliminates Faith. Acts 7: 55, "But he, being full of the Holy Ghost, looked up stedfastly into heaven, and saw the glory of God, and Jesus standing on the right hand of God."

3. Final Authority with Christ. I Cor. 15: 25, "For he must reign, till he hath put all enemies under his feet."

4. Heresy is Doomed Finally. I John 4: 1, "Beloved, believe not every spirit, but try the spirits whether they are of God."

POWER OF CHRISTIANITY

1. Survival of Christianity (Empires and civilizations have fallen). Matt. 16: 18, "Upon this rock I will build my church; and the gates of hell shall not prevail against it."

2. Survival of Faith (Common folk have maintained it). I Cor. 1: 27, "But God hath chosen the foolish things of the world to confound the wise."

3. Survival of Life (Christianity has always strengthened life). John 10: 10, "I am come that they might have life, and that they might have it more abundantly."

4. Survival of Witness (Many have fallen, others have been valiant). I Kings 19: 18, "Yet I have left me seven thousand in Israel, all the knees which have not bowed unto Baal."

Chapter XII

HYMN SERIES

In hymn series of sermons we are face to face with the same alternative as in the previous chapter. Most of our hymns are completely Biblical in concept and many of them are loaded with Scriptural language, yet to take a hymn for a sermon subject whether in a series or otherwise, and make it the basis of our exposition would be out of place for the Christian minister.

Many hymn series are possible if we will select such hymns carefully and then preach from a Bible text, using the particular hymn to expand on the divisions of the sermon as found in the text or as illustrating the truth of the text. Hymns are the precious heritage of God's people and we may make lawful use of them. A hymn series now and then will be very profitable but always such must be based on the word of God. The history of the hymn and of the writer of the hymn words can properly be moulded into the textual sermon if properly studied and presented. There is great possibility here but also great danger for the Christian minister. The examples listed in this chapter seek to give evidence of such proper balance so that the minister will always preach the word and use hymns to interest and challenge his people.

SALVATION THROUGH CHRIST

1. "Jesus Paid It All." Isa. 53: 6, "And the Lord hath laid on him the iniquity of us all."

2. "Saved by the Blood." Rom. 5: 9, "Being now justified by his blood, we shall be saved from wrath through him."

3. "Nearer, Still Nearer." Ps. 73: 28, "But it is good for me to draw near to God: I have put my trust in the Lord God."

4. "Grace, Enough for Me." Rom. 5: 17, "Much more they which receive abundance of grace and of the gift of righteousness shall reign in life by one, Jesus Christ."

5. "Crown Him With Many Crowns." Eph. 3: 21, "Unto him be glory in the church by Christ Jesus throughout all ages, world without end."

POSSESSIONS IN CHRIST

1. "Sweet Peace, The Gift of God's Love." John 14: 27, "Peace I leave with you, my peace I give unto you."

2. "What a Friend." John 15: 14, "Ye are my friends, if ye do whatsoever I command you."

3. "The Church's One Foundation." I Cor. 3: 11, "For other foundation can no man lay than that is laid, which is Jesus Christ."

4. "He Lifted Me." John 12: 32, "And I, if I be lifted up from the earth, will draw all men unto me."

5. "Christ Liveth in Me." Gal. 2: 20, "And the life which I now live in the flesh I live by the faith of the Son of God."

ASSURANCE OF SALVATION

1. "A Shelter in the Time of Storm." I Cor. 10: 4, "For they drank of that spiritual Rock that followed them: and that Rock was Christ."

2. "Blessed Assurance." Rom. 8: 16, "The Spirit itself beareth witness with our spirit, that we are the children of God."

3. "Hiding in Thee." Ps. 27: 5, "For in the time of trouble he shall hide me in his pavilion."

4. "He Will Hold Me Fast." John 10: 28, "And they shall never perish, neither shall any man pluck them out of my hand."

5. "I Know Whom I Have Believed." II Tim. 1: 12, "For I know whom I have believed, and am persuaded that he is able to keep that which I have committed unto him against that day."

SPIRITUAL PROTECTION

1. "Under His Wings." Ps. 91: 1, "He that dwelleth in the secret place of the most High shall abide under the shadow of the Almighty."

2. "We Have an Anchor." Heb. 6: 19, "Which hope we have as an anchor of the soul, both sure and stedfast."

3. "Just When I Need Him." Heb. 4: 15, "For we have not an high priest which cannot be touched with the feeling of our infirmities."

4. "The Lord Is My Shepherd." Ps. 23: 1, "The Lord is my shepherd; I shall not want."

5. "I Know That My Redeemer Liveth." John 9: 25, "One thing I know, that, whereas I was blind, now I see."

FELLOWSHIP WITH GOD

1. "He Leadeth Me." Ps. 23: 2, "He maketh me to lie down in green pastures: he leadeth me beside the still waters."

2. "Close to Thee." Ps. 73: 28, "But it is good for me to draw near to God: I have put my trust in the Lord God."

3. "Nearer My God to Thee." Gen. 28: 12, "And behold the angels of God ascending and descending on it."

4. "His Eye Is on the Sparrow." Ps. 84: 3, "Yea, the sparrow hath found an house, and the swallow a nest for herself."

5. "Faith Is the Victory." I John 5: 4, "And this is the victory that overcometh the world, even our faith."

WALKING WITH CHRIST

1. "O Master, Let Me Walk With Thee." Luke 24: 32, "Did not our heart burn within us, while he talked with us by the way?"

2. "Stepping in The Light." Phil. 3: 14, "I press toward the mark for the prize of the high calling of God in Christ Jesus."

3. "My Jesus, I Love Thee." John 21: 17, "Peter was grieved because he said unto him the third time, Lovest thou me?"

4. "There Is No Name So Sweet." Matt. 1: 21, "And thou shalt call his name Jesus: for he shall save his people from their sins."

5. "Victory Through Grace." I Peter 3: 7, "As being heirs together of the grace of life; that your prayers be not hindered."

PRAISE TO GOD

1. "Praise God, A Doxology." Ps. 103: 1, "Bless the Lord, O my soul: and all that is within me, bless his holy name."

2. "Fairest Lord Jesus." Song of Solomon 2: 1, "I am the rose of Sharon, and the lily of the valleys."

3. "Holy, Holy, Holy." II Cor. 13: 14, "The grace of the Lord Jesus Christ, and the love of God, and the communion of the Holy Ghost, be with you all."

4. "O Worship The King." Matt. 2: 2, "Where is he that is born King of Jews? . . . are come to worship him."

5. "For the Beauty of the Earth." Ps. 19: 1, "The heavens declare the glory of God; and the firmament sheweth his handywork."

PEACE OF GOD

1. "In Christ There is No East or West." Rom. 1: 16, "For I am not ashamed of the gospel of Christ; for it is the power of God unto salvation to everyone that believeth; to the Jew first, and also to the Greek."

2. "Wonderful Peace." John 15: 27, "And ye also shall bear witness, because ye have been with me from the beginning."

3. "It is Well With My Soul." Ps. 43: 5, "Why art thou cast down, O my soul? and why art thou disquieted within me?"

4. "Safe in the Arms of Jesus." John 10: 29, "And no man is able to pluck them out of my Father's hand."

5. "A Shelter in the Time of Storm." Ps. 46: 1, "God is our refuge and strength, a very present help in trouble."

I AM THINE, O LORD

1. "Closer Drawn to Thee." Ps. 73: 28, "But it is good for me to draw near to God: I have put my trust in the Lord God."

2. "Consecrate Me Now." Heb. 12: 1, "Let us lay aside every weight, and the sin which doth so easily beset us."

3. "O the Pure Delight." Ps. 19: 14, "Let the words of my mouth, and the meditation of my heart, be acceptable in thy sight, O Lord, my strength, and my redeemer."

4. "There Are Heights of Joy." I John 3: 2, "Beloved, now are we the sons of God, and it doth not yet appear what we shall be."

HOW FIRM A FOUNDATION

1. "How Firm A Foundation." II Tim. 2: 19, "Nevertheless the foundation of God standeth sure."

2. "Fear Not, I am With Thee." Matt. 28: 20b, "And, lo, I am with you alway, even unto the end of the world."

3. "Through Fiery Trials." Isa. 43: 2, "When thou passest through the waters, I will be with thee . . . when thou walkest through the fire, thou shalt not be burned."

4. "I Will Not Desert to His Foes." Matt. 16: 18, "And the gates of hell shall not prevail against it."

ONLY TRUST HIM

1. "Come Every Soul." Isa. 55: 1, "Ho, every one that thirsteth, come ye to the waters, and he that hath no money, come ye, buy, and eat."

2. "Jesus Shed His Precious Blood." I Cor. 11: 25, "This cup is the new testament in my blood."

3. "Jesus Is The Truth, The Way." John 14: 6, "Jesus saith unto him, I am the way, the truth, and the life."

4. "On to Glory Go." Ps. 84: 7, "They go from strength to strength, every one of them in Zion appeareth before God."

MY JESUS I LOVE THEE

1. "My Saviour Art Thou." I Tim. 4: 10, "Because we trust in the living God, who is the Saviour of all men."

2. "Thou Hast First Loved Me." I John 4: 19, "We love him, because he first loved us."

3. "I Will Praise Thee." Eph. 1: 6, "To the praise of the glory of his grace, wherein he hath made us accepted in the beloved."

4. "I Will Sing with the Glittering Crown on my Brow." Rev. 15: 3, "And they sing the song of Moses the servant of God, and the song of the Lamb."

COUNT YOUR BLESSINGS

1. "Name Them One by One." Ps. 103: 2, "Bless the Lord, O my soul, and forget not all his benefits."

2. "Burdened with a Load of Care." James 5: 7, "Be patient therefore, brethren, unto the coming of the Lord."

3. "Wealth Untold." I Cor. 3: 22-23. "All are yours; And ye are Christ's; and Christ is God's."

4. "Help and Comfort." John 14: 1, "Let not your heart be troubled: ye believe in God, believe also in me."

COME THOU ALMIGHTY KING

1. "Father All Glorious." Ps. 47: 6, "Sing praises to God, sing praises: sing praises unto our King."

2. "Come Thou Incarnate Word." John 1: 1, "In the beginning was the Word, and the Word was with God, and the Word was God."

3. "Come Holy Comforter." John 14: 26, "But the Comforter, which is the Holy Ghost, whom the Father will send in my name, he shall teach you all things."

4. "The Great One in Three." II Cor. 13: 14, "The grace of the Lord Jesus Christ, and the love of God, and the communion of the Holy Ghost, be with you all."

LOVE LIFTED ME

1. "I Was Sinking Deep in Sin." Matt. 14: 30, "But when he saw the wind boisterous, he was afraid; and beginning to sink, he cried, saying, Lord, save me."

2. "All My Heart to Him I'll Give." John 21: 17, "He said unto him, Lord, thou knowest all things; thou knowest that I love thee."

3. "Souls in Danger, Look Above." Acts 2: 28, "Thou hast made known to me the ways of life; thou shalt make me full of joy with thy countenance."

ONCE FOR ALL

1. "Free from the Law." Rom. 5: 18, "Even so by the righteousness of one the free gift came upon all men unto justification of life."

2. "No Condemnation." Rom. 8: 1, "There is therefore now no condemnation to them which are in Christ Jesus."

3. "Children of God." Rom. 8: 15, "But ye have received the Spirit of adoption, whereby we cry, Abba, Father."

HE LEADETH ME

1. "'Tis God's Hand that Leadeth Me." Ps. 31: 3, "For thou art my rock and my fortress; therefore for thy name's sake lead me, and guide me."

2. "O'er Troubled Sea." Ps. 46: 1, "God is our refuge and strength, a very present help in trouble."

3. "Content, Whatever Lot I See." Phil. 4: 11, "For I have learned, in whatsoever state I am, therewith to be content."

4. "Death's Cold Wave, I Will Not Flee." I Cor. 15: 57, "But thanks be to God, which giveth us the victory through our Lord Jesus Christ."

GIVE ME THY HEART

1. "Says the Father Above." Matt. 22: 37, "Jesus said unto him, Thou shalt love the Lord thy God with all thy heart, and with all thy soul, and with all thy mind."

2. "Says the Saviour of Men." Luke 21: 14, "Settle it therefore in your hearts, not to meditate before what ye shall answer."

3. "Says the Spirit Divine." I Peter 3: 15, "Sanctify the Lord God in your hearts: and be ready always to give an answer to every man."

WHOSOEVER WILL

1. "Whosoever Heareth." John 5: 25, "The hour is coming, and now is, when the dead shall hear the voice of the Son of God: and they that hear shall live."

2. "Whosoever Cometh." Isa. 55: 1, "Ho, every one that thirsteth, come ye to the waters, and he that hath no money; come ye, buy, and eat."

3. "Whosoever Will." John 3: 16, "Whosoever believeth in him should not perish, but have everlasting life."

Chapter XIII
NATURE SERIES

God has revealed Himself in two books, the book of revelation and the Word of God and the book of nature. The realm of nature in the light of the Scriptures affords many serial suggestions which can be properly used by the minister for sermonic usage.

There are seasons of the year of which we are all conscious and these can be used with Bible emphasis to glorify God and edify those who listen to serial nature sermons. The locality where we live makes a big difference. The city dweller will not appreciate nature series as much as those who live on the farm. Here is a field rich for spiritual cultivation in the word of God and in the approach of nature series of sermons.

NATURE REVEALS GOD

1. Nature Reveals God's Providence. Matt. 6: 26, "Behold the fowls of the air: for they sow not, neither do they reap, nor gather into barns; yet your heavenly Father feedeth them."

2. Nature Reveals God's Work. John 5: 17, "But Jesus answered them, My Father worketh hitherto, and I work."

3. Nature Reveals God's Power. Ps. 135: 5, "For I know that the Lord is great, and that our Lord is above all gods."

4. Nature Reveals God's Goodness. Ps. 104: 14, "He causeth the grass to grow for the cattle, and the herb for the service of man."

5. Nature Reveals God's Creation. Gen. 1: 1, "In the beginning God created the heaven and the earth."

6. Nature Reveals God's Revelation. Rom. 1: 20, "For the invisible things of him from the creation of the world are clearly seen."

SIGNIFICANT TREES

1. The Forbidden Tree. Gen. 2: 17, "But of the tree of the knowledge of good and evil, thou shalt not eat of it."

2. The Sycamine Tree Luke 17: 6, "Ye might say unto this sycamine tree, Be thou plucked up by the root, and be thou planted in the sea; and it should obey you."

3. The Fig Tree. Luke 21: 29, "And he spake to them a parable; Behold the fig tree, and all the trees."

4. The Good Tree. Matt. 7: 18, "A good tree cannot bring forth evil fruit, neither can a corrupt tree bring forth good fruit."

5. The Green Tree. Luke 23: 31, "For if they do these things in a green tree, what shall be done in the dry?"

6. The Cursed Tree. Gal. 3: 13, "Cursed is every one that hangeth on a tree."

7. The Tree of Life. Rev. 22: 2, "Was there the tree of life, which bare twelve manner of fruits."

PLANTING LESSONS

1. A Branch of God's Planting. Isa. 60: 21, "Thy people also shall be all righteous . . . the branch of my planting, the work of my hands."

2. A Planted Vineyard. Deut. 28: 30, "Thou shalt plant a vineyard, and shalt not gather the grapes thereof."

3. A Planted Tree. Ps. 1: 3, "And he shall be like a tree planted by the rivers of water."

4. Planted Together. Rom. 6: 5, "For if we have been planted together in the likeness of his death, we shall be also in the likeness of his resurrection."

5. Planting Growth. I Cor. 3: 6, "I have planted, Apollos watered; but God gave the increase."

BIBLE FLOWERS

1. Consider the Lilies. Matt. 6: 28, "Consider the lilies of the field, how they grow; they toil not, neither do they spin."

2. The Fading Flower. Isa. 40: 7, "The grass withereth, the flower fadeth: but the word of our God shall stand for ever."

3. The Lily of the Valley. Song of Solomon 2: 1, "I am the rose of Sharon, and the lily of the valleys."

4. An Olive Flower. Job 15: 33, "And shall cast off his flower as the olive."

MANIFESTATIONS OF NATURE

1. Creation. Gen. 1: 1, "In the beginning God created the heaven and the earth."

2. Rain, the Gift of God. Matt. 5: 45, "And sendeth rain on the just and on the unjust."

3. Created Stars. Gen. 1: 16, "And God made two great lights; the greater light to rule the day, and the lesser light to rule the night: he made the stars also."

4. The Rainbow of Promise. Gen. 9: 13, "I do set my bow in the cloud, and it shall be for a token of a covenant between me and the earth."

5. Day and Night. Gen. 8: 22, "While the earth remaineth, seedtime and harvest, cold and heat, and summer and winter, and day and night shall not cease."

6. Sun of Righteousness. Mal. 4: 2, "But unto you that fear my name shall the Sun of righteousness arise with healing in his wings."

LESSONS FROM THE STARS

1. Created Stars. Gen. 1: 16, "He made the stars also."

2. Worship of Stars. Deut. 4: 19, "And lest thou lift up thine eyes unto heaven, and when thou seest the sun, and the moon, and the stars, even all the host of heaven, shouldest be driven to worship them."

3. The Star of Christ's Birth. Matt. 2: 2, "For we have seen his star in the east, and are come to worship him."

4. Stars as a Multitude. Heb. 11: 12, "So many as the stars of the sky in multitude."

GOD'S GLORY IN NATURE – PSALM 19

1. The Firmament Sheweth God's Handywork. Vs. 1, "The heavens declare the glory of God; and the firmament sheweth his handywork."

2. Day and Night. Vs. 2, "Day unto day uttereth speech, and night unto night sheweth knowledge."

3. All the Earth. Vs. 4, "Their line is gone out through all the earth, and their words to the end of the world."

4. The End of Heaven. Vs. 7, "The law of the Lord is perfect, converting the soul: the testimony of the Lord is sure, making wise the simple."

5. Honey and the Honeycomb. Vs. 10, "More to be desired are they than gold, yea, than much fine gold: sweeter also than honey and the honeycomb."

IMPORTANT RIVERS OF THE BIBLE

1. The River of Damascus. II Kings 5: 12, "Are not Abana and Pharpar, rivers of Damascus, better than all the waters of Israel?"

2. The River of God. Ps. 65: 9, "Thou visitest the earth, and waterest it: thou greatly enrichest it with the river of God, which is full of water."

3. The River of Babylon. Ps. 137: 1, "By the rivers of Babylon, there we sat down, yes, we wept, when we remembered Zion."

4. The River of Adoption. Ex. 2: 10, "And she called his name Moses: and she said, Because I drew him out of the water."

5. The River of Blood. Ex. 7: 17, "I will smite with the rod that is in mine hand upon the waters which are in the river, and they shall be turned to blood."

6. The River of Baptism. Luke 3: 3, "And he came into all the country about Jordan, preaching the baptism of repentance for the remission of sins."

7. The River of Life. Rev. 22: 1, "And he shewed me a pure river of water of life, clear as crystal."

LESSONS FROM STONES

1. Stones Turned Into Bread. Luke 4: 3, "If thou be the Son of God, command this stone that it be made bread."

2. By Interpretation, A Stone. John 1: 42, "Thou art Simon the son of Jona: thou shalt be called Cephas, which is by interpretation, A stone."

3. The Rejected Stone. Matt. 21: 42, "The stone which the builders rejected, the same is become the head of the corner."

4. The Rolled Away Stone. Luke 24: 2, "And they found the stone rolled away from the sepulchre."

5. Lively Stones. I Peter 2: 5, "Ye also, as lively stones, are built up a spiritual house."

6. Precious Stones. Rev. 2: 17, "And will give him a white stone, and in the stone a new name written."

LESSONS FROM THE CLOUDS

1. A Little Cloud. I Kings 18: 44, "Behold, there ariseth a little cloud out of the sea, like a man's hand."

2. A Speaking Cloud. Ps. 99: 7, "He spake unto them in the cloudy pillar: they kept his testimonies."

3. A Thick Cloud. Isa. 44: 22, "I have blotted out, as a thick cloud, thy transgressions."

4. A Power Cloud. Luke 21: 27, "And then shall they see the Son of man coming in a cloud with power and great glory."

5. An Empty Cloud. Jude 12, "Clouds they are without water, carried about of winds. . . ."

6. A White Cloud. Rev. 14: 14, "And I looked, and behold a white cloud, and upon the cloud one sat like unto the Son of man."

WISDOM FROM THE WIND

1. Windy Speech. Job 6: 26, "Do ye imagine to reprove words, and the speeches of one that is desperate, which are as wind?"

2. Life as Wind. Job 7: 7, "O remember that my life is wind: mine eye shall no more see good."

3. Inheriting the Wind. Prov. 11: 29, "He that troubleth his own house shall inherit the wind."

4. Created Wind. Amos 4: 13, "For, lo, he that formeth the mountains, and createth the wind, and declareth unto man what is his thought."

5. A Wind Shaken Reed. Matt. 11: 7, "What went ye out into the wilderness to see? A reed shaken with the wind?"

6. Example of Wind. John 3: 8 "The wind bloweth where it listeth, and thou heareth the sound thereof, but canst not tell whence it cometh, and whither it goeth."

7. Windy Doctrine. Eph. 4: 14, "That we henceforth be no more children, tossed to and fro, and carried about with every wind of doctrine.

8. A Rebuked Wind. Matt. 8: 26, "And rebuked the winds and the sea; and there was a great calm."

SIGNS IN NATURE

1. Sign of Sun and Moon. Gen. 1: 14, "And God said, Let there be lights in the firmament of the heaven to divide the day from the night."

2. Sign of the Rainbow. Gen. 9: 13, "I do set my bow in the cloud, and it shall be for a token of a covenant between me and the earth."

3. Sign of the Fleece. Judg. 6: 37, "Behold, I will put a fleece of wool in the floor."

4. Sign of the Pillar. Ex. 13: 21, "And the Lord went before them by day in a pillar of a cloud, to lead them the way."

HARVESTS OF GOD

1. A Promised Harvest. Gen. 8: 22, "While the earth remaineth, seedtime and harvest, and cold and heat, and summer and winter, and day and night shall not cease."

2. A Past Harvest. Jer. 8: 20, "The harvest is past, the summer is ended, and we are not saved."

3. A Great Harvest. Luke 10: 2, "The harvest truly is great, but the labourers are few."

4. A White Harvest. John 4: 35, "Lift up your eyes, and look on the fields; for they are white already to harvest."

5. A Final Harvest. Matt. 13: 30, "And in the time of harvest I will say to the reapers, Gather ye together first the tares, and bind them in bundles to burn them."

LESSONS FROM SHADOWS

1. Life Like a Shadow. Ps. 102: 11, "My days are like a shadow that declineth; and I am withered like grass."

2. Under the Shadow of God. Ps. 91: 1, "He that dwelleth in the secret place of the most High shall abide under the shadow of the Almighty."

3. No Shadow of Turning. James 1: 17, "Every good and every perfect gift is from above, and cometh down from the Father of lights, with whom is no variableness, neither shadow of turning."

4. Shadow of Heavenly Things. Heb. 8: 5, "Who serve unto the example and shadow of heavenly things."

IMPORTANT MOUNTS

1. Ararat, Resting of the Ark. Gen. 8: 4

2. Carmel, Elijah's Sacrifice. I Kings 18: 19

3. Gerizim, Site of Samaritan Temple. John 4: 20
4. Hermon, Conjectured Site of the Transfiguration. Deut. 4: 48
5. Horeb, Burning Bush. Ex. 3: 1
6. Lebanon, Source of wood for Temple. II Chron. 2: 8-10
7. Moriah, Place of Abraham's Sacrifice. Gen. 22: 2
8. Olivet, Place of Christ's Ascension. Acts 1: 9-12
9. Sinai, Place of Giving the Law. Ex. 19: 1-11
10. Zion, Site of David's Palace. II Sam. 5: 7